Jobs-Housing Balance

Jerry Weitz, AICP

TABLE OF CONTENTS

Jobs-Housing Balance

Trends show that people are driving more places at longer distances. As shown in Table 1, vehicle trip lengths in the United States over the past three decades have fluctuated some but have generally increased for all trip purposes.

Work trips as of 1995 were the longest of all trip purposes. This represents an opportunity for planners. By planning communities with better balances of jobs and housing units, we can shorten work trips and thereby have a significant impact on vehicle miles traveled.

TABLE 1
AVERAGE VEHICLE TRIP LENGTH IN MILES BY PURPOSE OF TRIP:
1969, 1977, 1983, 1990, AND 1995, UNITED STATES

Trip Purpose	1969	1977	1983	1990	1995
To/from work	9.40	9.02	8.55	10.97	11.80
For family and personal business	6.51	6.72	6.68	7.43	6.93
For shopping	4.36	4.99	5.28	5.10	5.64
For social and recreation	13.12	10.27	10.55	11.80	11.24
For all purposes	8.90	8.35	7.90	8.85	9.06

Source: Nationwide Personal Transportation Survey (2000)

Land-use patterns—which have increased travel distances because of the separation of homes, jobs, and other destinations—can be blamed for approximately one-third of the increase in driving. Better-planned mixed-use communities with balanced jobs and housing can help reduce travel distances and thus limit the growth in trip lengths (Urban Land Institute 1999). These better-planned communities can also provide additional benefits, including a reduction in the amount of land developed overall to meet the needs of growing populations as well as greater efficiency in the provision and use of public infrastructure and services.

Any increase in commuting trips and distances costs all of us money. Let's take a look at four hypothetical workers: Robert, Amy, Jason, and Kathy. Robert works at home and thus has no commuting costs (see Table 2). Amy found an apartment close to her job and has a short commute. Jason purchased a house that is an approximately equal distance between his and his wife's workplaces; his commute is moderate in terms of distance, time, and cost. Because Kathy wanted a house but could not afford any close to her workplace, she purchased one in an area far from her employer. As shown in Table 2, Kathy's total annual commute costs are more than three times those of Amy. And while Amy spends only 3.5 minutes on the road for every hour she works, Kathy spends 12.

Kathy may not realize it, but her decision to live far from her job marginally increases the driving times and costs of all other drivers . . . hundreds or thousands of Kathys can significantly increase traffic congestion and air pollution in the region.

TABLE 2
COMMUTING CHARACTERISTICS OF FOUR HYPOTHETICAL WORKERS

Data	Robert Works At Home	Amy Works Close To Home	Jason Works Moderately Near Home	Kathy Works Far From Home
One-way vehicle miles traveled to work	0	6	11	22
One-way peak travel time to work (minutes)	0	14	26	48
Travel cost per one-way trip to work (@ $0.345 per mile)	$0	$2.07	$3.80	$7.59
Annual travel cost of round trips to work (260 work days)	$0	$1,076	$1,976	$3,947
Annual hours commuting to and from work	0	121	225	416
Annual cost of commute to and from work (@ $12.40 per hour)	$0	$1,500	$2,790	$5,158
Total annual cost of commute (travel plus commute time)	$0	$2,576	$4,766	$9,105

Note: Mileage cost of $0.345 per mile was an accepted federal standard for mileage reimbursement as of 2001. The 260 workdays measure is based on an eight-hour day and the generally accepted standard of 2,080 hours annually per employee. The annual cost of commute to work of $12.40 per hour is used by the Texas Transportation Institute (2001).

Despite her high commute costs, Kathy is likely saving money since her housing costs are less than they might have been had she purchased a home or rented an apartment close to her workplace. She may also benefit from the intangible benefits that come from homeownership, including personal satisfaction. However, as more and more people like Kathy make the same decision to live far from their workplaces, the cumulative impacts become much greater. Kathy may not realize it, but her decision marginally increases the driving times and costs of all other drivers. And hundreds or thousands of Kathys can significantly increase traffic congestion and air pollution in the region.

In recent decades, more and more people like Kathy have been unable to live close to their jobs because such housing does not exist or is too expensive. The Atlanta region is a good case in point. Vehicle miles traveled (VMT) there have increased substantially over recent years, and at much faster rates than population growth (see Table 3). For every person in the Atlanta region, there were 35.1 miles driven daily in 1999, up about 77 percent from 1982.

TABLE 3
VEHICLE MILES TRAVELED (VMT) AND POPULATION ATLANTA REGION, 1982–1999

	1982	1990	1982–1990 Percent Increase	1999	1990–1999 Percent Increase
Daily VMT	31,925,000	61,185,000	91.6	100,460,000	64.2
Total Population (including those that do not drive)	1,610,000	2,100,000	30.4	2,860,000	36.2
Daily VMT Per Person	19.8	29.1	47.0	35.1	20.6

Source: Texas Transportation Institute (2001)

The continued increase in VMT in the Atlanta region has been accompanied by other disturbing trends. The region's low-income and minority workers are now spatially isolated from employment opportunities. The lack of affordable housing in or near employment centers "leads to long commutes on crowded freeways" for the region's workers (Brookings Institution 2000, 6). A "severe jobs-housing imbalance" exists in the city's northern suburbs, and "the housing deficit also worsens the area's congestion problems by forcing families to travel long distances to their places of employment. Additionally, the housing imbalance places enormous stresses on the region's employers by limiting the pool of workers who can live within a reasonable commuting distance" (Brookings Institution 2000, 20). Atlanta's low-density housing and dispersed, low-intensity employment areas increase the hours commuters spend in their cars and thus contribute to the region's miserable air pollution record (Brookings Institution 2000).

Atlanta's low-density housing and dispersed, low-intensity employment areas increase the hours commuters spend in their cars and thus contribute to the region's miserable air pollution record.

THE STORY OF MARZS MATA

Noah Adams, a reporter for National Public Radio, did a series of reports for NPR on "One Town, One Job: Low-Wage America" that involved a two-week driving trip on Interstate 75 from Knoxville, Tennessee, to Detroit, Michigan. In Detroit, Adams talked with Marzs Mata, who works for ComCast customer service in a Detroit suburb. In an essay appearing on NPR's web site, Adams describes how he met Mata and what her commute is like. Marzs Mata's story makes issues about jobs-housing balance very real in a very personal way.

"That night we went to a meeting of transit riders, organized to push for better city and suburban bus service. And we left with a phone number for Marzs Mata, a commuter (who couldn't make the evening meeting because her bus ride home takes too long). Mata is one of thousands who travel each day from Detroit's old neighborhoods downtown out to the suburbs, where the new jobs are. Mostly the work is entry-level and low-wage. Anne called Mata at 10 that night to ask if we could ride along the following evening.

Marzs Mata's three-bus commute home was nearly three hours long. We have all of it on tape; only a couple of minutes were used in our report. It was a strange and sad evening, but uplifting as well. She is 50 years old, has never had a driver's license, or owned a car. Not all that long ago, she was hitchhiking around California with a guitar, a knapsack, a few dollars and some oranges. Now, after being on welfare, she's been through computer training and has a promising future—if she can just hold on."

An audio file of the NPR *Morning Edition* story about Ms. Mata is available at http://www.npr.org/news/specials/low_wage/index.html. Noah Adams's essay is available at: http://www.npr.org/news/specials/low_wage/essay.html.

Atlanta's jobs-housing imbalances are partially to blame for greater commute distances, times, and costs. But Atlanta is hardly unique. If trends there hold true elsewhere in the United States, the continued nationwide increase in VMT should be a cause for concern among planners. Business owners, elected officials, and planners should recognize that a mismatch between housing and jobs adds not only to the commuting costs of most people; it also costs them time with their family and the potential for greater involvement in their community, increases the cost of government services and infrastructure, can negatively affect the future economic vitality of the region, and creates stress that can lead to lost productivity. To minimize these costs, local policies and regulations should allow some residents, like Robert, to work out of their homes. Localities should also provide opportunities for everyone who wants to live moderately close to their jobs to do so. If given the choice, might not Jason and his wife consider living even closer to their workplaces? Wouldn't we all benefit from having Kathy live closer to her job?

Planners who prepare comprehensive plans, administer zoning ordinances, and review large-scale developments can use this report to implement policies aimed at promoting jobs-housing balance.

OVERVIEW OF JOBS-HOUSING BALANCE

Jobs-housing balance is a planning tool that local governments can use to achieve a roughly equal number of jobs and housing units (or households) in a jurisdiction. The notion of balancing jobs and housing goes well beyond trying to attain numerical equality. Ideally, the jobs available in a community should match the labor force skills, and housing should be available at prices, sizes, and locations suited to workers who wish to live in the area. Hence, there is a qualitative as well as quantitative component to achieving jobs-housing balance. Jobs-housing balance is a planning technique rather than a regulatory tool. Nonetheless, this report demonstrates the various ways that the concept of jobs-housing balance can be applied in local land-use regulations and large-scale development reviews.

A ratio of jobs to housing is most commonly used to express the concept of jobs-housing balance. Generally and simply stated, the jobs-housing ratio is a ratio between a measure of employment and a measure of housing in a given area of analysis. The most basic measure is the ratio of the number of jobs to the number of housing units in an area. To calculate this measure, divide the number of jobs by the number of housing units. For example, if 15,000 persons are employed in a city and 20,000 housing units exist, the city's jobs-housing unit ratio is 15,000/20,000 = 0.75.

What jobs-housing standard should be used, and what should the benchmark be? Table 4 provides common targets and target ranges for two jobs-housing measurements.

TABLE 4 COMMON JOBS: HOUSING MEASUREMENTS AND STANDARDS Jobs-Housing Measurement	Recommended Target Standard (Implies Balance)	Recommended Target Range (Implies Balance)	Reference
Jobs to housing units ratio	1.5 : 1	1.3 : 1 to 1.7 : 1 or 1.4 : 1 to 1.6 : 1	Ewing 1996; Cervero 1991
Jobs to employed residents ratio	1 : 1	0.8 : 1 to 1.25 : 1	Cervero 1996

The recommended target standard and ranges for jobs-housing unit ratios are based on the assumption that the average number of workers per household is approximately 1.5. But this number can vary from community to community. Some households have two or more workers, while others have none. If possible, the standard should be based on an analysis of local data on workers per household. If communities try to match working residents (labor force) with employment in the community, a one-to-one (1:1) relationship is the ideal.

Typology of Jobs-Housing Imbalances

This report will analyze four possible types of imbalances of jobs and housing, as summarized in Table 5. Imbalances can differ depending on geographic location within a region (see Figure 1). The policies proposed can also differ depending on the type of jobs-housing imbalance.

TABLE 5. TYPOLOGY OF JOBS-HOUSING IMBALANCES

Type of Imbalance	Jobs	Housing Units	Example
Type 1	Too many low-wage	Too few low-end	Suburban employment centers [or: edge cities]
Type 2	Too many high-wage	Too few high-end	Downtown employment areas in central cities
Type 3	Too few low-wage	Too much low-end	Older suburbs and central-city neighborhoods
Type 4	Too few high-wage	Too much high-end	High-income bedroom communities

Type 1: The area is job-rich and needs more housing for low-wage workers. A city or county with lots of entry-level retail and service jobs but little or no low- to moderate-income housing might find it needs to correct its jobs-housing imbalance with a policy that ensures housing meets the price ranges of moderately skilled, low-wage workers. These imbalances are probably most likely to occur in suburban job centers. The provision of affordable housing within or close to the job center is needed to address this imbalance.

Type 2: The area is job-rich and needs more housing for executives, managers, and professionals (i.e., higher-wage workers). A community might find that it needs more high-end residences to house corporate executives and similar high-income professionals. Shortages of high-end housing are rare, however, because there is high market demand and developers achieve high profits from new subdivisions targeted at these professionals. In other words, market response is generally adequate to prevent frequent Type 2 jobs-housing imbalances. Where these imbalances are more likely to occur is in the downtown area of a central city (e.g., a banking, finance, and governmental center of a region), which for a variety of reasons (e.g., a lack of amenities, perceptions that public schools are inadequate, concerns about crime) has not established a residential market.

The policy responses appropriate to addressing a Type 2 jobs-housing imbalance will depend on the particular characteristics of the area. Planners addressing Type 2 imbalances should begin with an analysis of the likely reasons that market-rate housing has not been built.

Type 3: The area is job-poor and needs more employment opportunities for the resident, lower-wage, labor force. Planners might find that the area under investigation is predominantly residential, housing low-wage workers who don't have employment opportunities close by that match their skills. Type 3 jobs-housing imbalances beg for an "economic development" solution that brings lower-skilled jobs into or near the neighborhoods of lower-income resident workers.

Shortages of high-end housing are rare because there is high market demand and developers achieve high profits from new subdivisions targeted at these professionals.

PASSING EACH OTHER ON THE ROAD
IN SOUTHERN WILLAMETTE VALLEY, OREGON

Coburg, Oregon, is a small, rural community approximately seven miles north of Eugene in Lane County. Coburg has ample industrial employment along I-5, which skirts its western edge. The city had 1,704 jobs and 388 housing units in 1998; its jobs-to-housing units ratio was therefore 4.39 to 1 (Lane Council of Governments 2000). Studies of travel behavior conducted by the city of Coburg and the Lane Transit District illustrate the nature of Coburg's mismatch of jobs and residences:

- Among Coburg residents, 96 percent of workers or students commuted outside the Coburg area to work or school; only 4 percent of the respondents said they work in the Coburg area.

- Among workers in Coburg's industrial and highway commercial areas, 97 percent said they live outside the Coburg area.

These studies reflect the fact that there is not enough affordable housing in Coburg for the workers employed there. New single-family housing being constructed in Coburg is priced in the $200,000 to $400,000 range. Coburg's employment and housing characteristics illustrate a severe Type 1 jobs-housing imbalance.

Other small municipalities in the Eugene-Springfield Metropolitan Statistical Area have entirely different conditions. A number of small cities have more housing units than jobs. Homes in these small cities have substantially lower values than those in Eugene, which had an average value of $138,100 in 1996.

The more affordable homes in these smaller cities suggest that they are attractive to moderately skilled, low-wage workers (such as those who work in Coburg). These small cities illustrate a Type 3 jobs-housing imbalance.

Together, the jobs-rich, housing-deficient city of Coburg and the jobs-poor, housing-rich cities of Creswell, Oakridge, Veneta, and Lowell illustrate the significant imbalances that currently exist in the Southern Willamette Valley region. According to the Oregon Department of Transportation's report *Commuting in the Willamette Valley*, "the dispersion of jobs and housing has resulted in increased commuting within and between cities in the Willamette Valley, predominantly within a 30-minute commute distance of major employment centers" (quoted in Lane Council of Governments 2000, 7).

TABLE 6
COMPARISON OF SMALL CITIES IN THE
SOUTHERN WILLAMETTE VALLEY, OREGON

City	Employment (1998)	Housing Units (1998)	Jobs-Housing Housing Unit Ratio (1998)	Average Housing Value (1996)
Creswell	991	1,396	0.71	$83,400
Oakridge	707	1,762	0.40	$65,900
Veneta	544	1,166	0.47	$99,300
Lowell	148	380	0.39	$65,600

Source: Lane Council of Governments (2000)

Type 4: The area is job-poor but has a highly skilled resident labor force. This type of situation would appear to be rare but is in fact common in many middle- and higher-income suburban parts of a region. This type of mismatch between residences and jobs is likely to result primarily from public policy (i.e., local land-use policy) decisions to maintain an area's predominantly residential character. If not constrained by policies that "zone-out" employment in order to maintain a bedroom community, the market is likely to correct this imbalance over time: employers study the strength of the local labor force in terms of their skills and education levels, and under many conditions will be eager to locate close to pools of skilled labor force. A change in local land-use policies (i.e., zoning for more employment) is the best policy response to this type of imbalance.

EDGE CITY:
A TYPE 1 JOBS-HOUSING IMBALANCE

Peripheral clusters of activity in a metropolitan area, known as edge cities (Garreau 1991), bring together a mix of activities at a scale somewhere between central cities and low-density suburbs. Edge cities, which are spread across the United States, are major employment centers and entertainment nodes. They are also supposed to be self-contained, allowing people to live, work, and consume in the same place (Beauregard 1995).

By definition, however, edge cities are imbalanced. Joel Garreau (1991) has defined an edge city as having, among other characteristics, more jobs than bedrooms. A high degree of social homogeneity and exclusion occurs in edge cities, whose populations are predominantly white and middle class. Likewise, Robert A. Beauregard notes, "traffic congestion is irritating and hinders mobility, housing is expensive, [and] low-wage workers often are hard to find . . ." (Beauregard 1995, 712). The most pressing question that edge cities face, therefore, is whether they can overcome this Type 1 jobs-housing imbalance: "Can edge cities manage the contradiction between their need for low-wage workers in retail, entertainment, and personal services and for police and fire personnel, and the lack of affordable housing?" (Beauregard 1995, 716).

The Consequences of Jobs-Housing Imbalances

In areas where public transportation is not available and workplaces are located significant distances from neighborhoods, the only realistic alternative for workers who cannot work from home is to commute by car to their job location. The spatial mismatch between the locations of jobs and

FIGURE 1. FOUR TYPES OF JOBS-HOUSING-IMBALANCED AREAS IN A REGION RESULT IN LONGER COMMUTE TRIPS

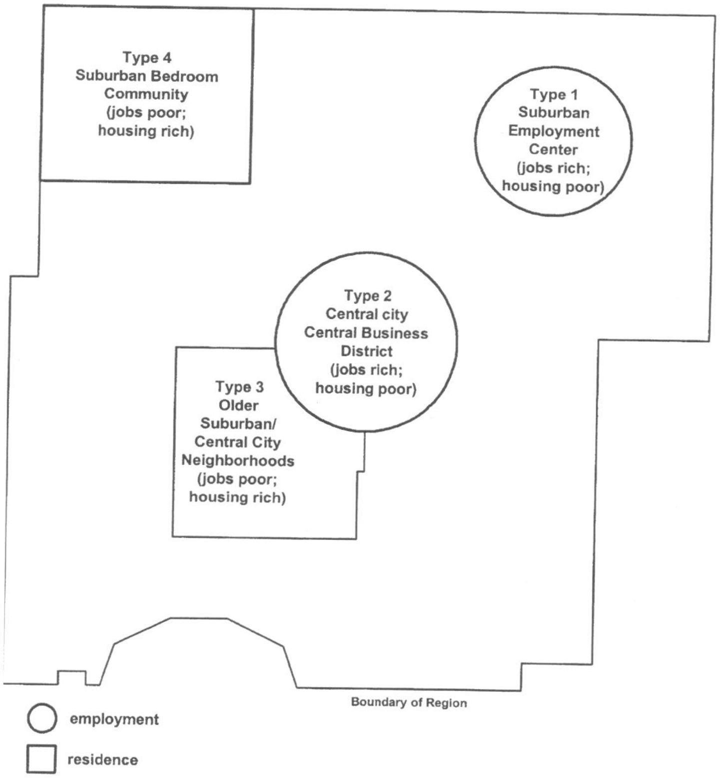
Type 4
Suburban Bedroom Community
(jobs poor; housing rich)
Type 1
Suburban Employment Center
(jobs rich; housing poor)
Type 2
Central city Central Business District
(jobs rich; housing poor)
Type 3
Older Suburban/ Central City Neighborhoods
(jobs poor; housing rich)
Boundary of Region
employment
residence

housing (see Figure 1) is considered one important reason for the longer commute trips and deteriorating traffic conditions in many metropolitan regions. When numerous employees live far from their work places and have to drive to work, the result is often longer commutes and greater vehicle miles traveled. Traffic congestion, increased driver frustrations, reduced worker productivity, poor air quality, and reduced quality of life can also occur as a result of such imbalances.

What Planners Can Do

Communities are increasingly realizing that their land-use plans and regulations have a major influence on whether workers can arrive at their job location on time and whether workers even have the choice of living close to their jobs. Planners must begin to address jobs-housing imbalances in their communities by investigating the types of mismatches that exist between the types of jobs in an area and the types and cost of housing. Understanding the four types of jobs-housing imbalances described above will help planners and policy makers to formulate appropriate policy responses. Each of the imbalances, however, is best addressed by providing better balances of jobs and housing in several different parts of the region or locality (see Figure 2). While correcting just one jobs-housing imbalance in a region can have benefits, the result of multiple jobs-housing balancing efforts throughout a region can be shorter commute trips and, in sum, a broad reversal of the negative consequences of imbalance.

FIGURE 2. A MORE BALANCED DISTRIBUTION OF JOBS AND HOUSING SHORTENS COMMUTE TRIPS

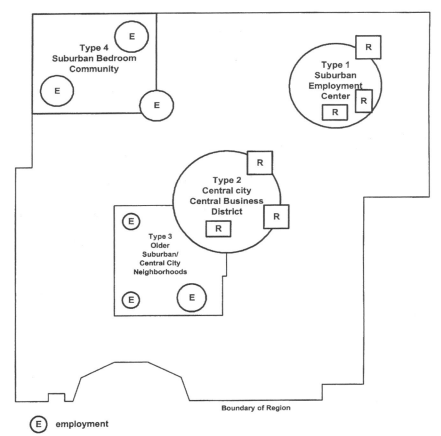

WHAT WE KNOW AND DON'T KNOW

Jobs-housing imbalances are widespread within large U.S. metropolitan areas (Downs 1992). But can a jobs-housing balance policy actually reduce vehicle miles traveled (VMT) in those areas? It may seem self-evident that bringing jobs and housing closer together in terms of distance and quality will likely result in fewer miles driven to work and for other trip purposes. But there are those who disagree with the contention that jobs-housing balance will provide remedies for the urban and metropolitan ills caused by excessive VMT, such as traffic congestion and poor air quality. This section of the report summarizes both sides of the debate and presents available evidence regarding the usefulness of jobs-housing balancing policies.

Jobs-Housing Balance Promotes Smart Growth

Any policy that seeks to balance jobs and housing has multiple objectives, but almost all of these objectives will promote smart growth. The leading scholar on the concept of jobs-housing balance, Robert Cervero (1989; 1991), suggests that jobs-housing balance policies can help to reduce urban sprawl and lower energy consumption. The most important objectives of jobs-housing balance policies, in the eyes of those who have implemented them, have been the reduction of VMT and other traffic impacts.

Reduced congestion and lower VMT. Severe jobs-housing imbalances have been shown to result in high levels of freeway congestion (Cervero 1989). Where jobs and housing are close geographically and numerically in a given area or community, workers have the opportunity to drive shorter distances, which should reduce average trip lengths and thereby reduce VMT (Ewing 1996).

There is evidence that intensifying housing in downtown areas can reduce peak-hour commute trips into those areas. David M. Nowlan and Greg Stewart (1991), for example, studied commuting to Toronto's central downtown and concluded that inbound trips had been reduced due to the increase in residential population there. The authors estimate that "for each 100 additional dwelling units in the Central Area there has been a reduction of approximately 120 inbound trips during the morning three-hour rush period" (Nowlan and Stewart 1991, 165).

In a study of the Greater Seattle-Tacoma region, Lawrence Frank and Gary Pivo (1994) found that travel distances tend to be shorter for commutes to balanced areas (see also Cervero 1996). The San Diego Association of Government's Regional Growth Management Strategy (1991) found that commute trip lengths in sectors with balanced jobs and housing were 8.8 miles, two miles less than the regional average (Ewing 1996, 46, n. 17).

The Southern California Association of Government (SCAG) provides additional evidence of VMT reduction from implementing jobs-housing balancing policies. In its report, *The New Economy and Jobs/Housing Balance in Southern California* (Armstrong and Sears 2001, 19), SCAG finds:

> The opportunity to live close to the workplace afforded by providing housing close to well-paying jobs translates to lower congestion and commute times by eliminating the necessity for long-distance commutes . . . [SCAG's strategy of redistributing] 9 percent of the region's forecast employment growth to the year 2010 from job-rich to job-poor areas, and 5 percent of the forecast housing growth from housing-rich to housing-poor areas . . . was estimated to reduce regional vehicle miles traveled (VMT) by 33.4 million miles (8.5 percent). . . .

In Portland, Oregon, in the mid-1990s, the regional government Metro modeled different scenarios for future growth as part of its Region 2040 process. It found that growing without expansion of the Portland region

---

urban growth boundary would have the lowest VMT per capita when compared to a base case wherein existing expansion trends continued and to other growth concepts. It also found that a "satellite city" concept that funneled one-third of the region's growth into neighboring cities had lower VMT per capita than the base case (Metro 1994a; 1994b). See also Region 2040 in the Applications section of this PAS Report.

Reduced travel time and lower personal transportation costs. Some simulations have shown that transportation costs can be reduced significantly if employment is dispersed among residential areas in a metropolitan area instead of concentrated in a central location surrounded by residences (Altshuler and Gomez-Ibanez 1993). Cervero (1989) provides limited evidence that jobs-housing mismatches can lead to more-time-consuming commutes.

Travel time can be less in communities that have a jobs-housing balance than in communities that are unbalanced. Unpublished research (Weitz and Schindler 1997; see Weitz 1999) has calculated jobs-housing ratios for cities and census-designated places (CDPs) in Oregon. That research was conducted to determine if those communities with jobs-housing balances had shorter commute times than communities with jobs-housing imbalances. Balanced communities were determined to be those cities and CDPs with a ratio of jobs to households within the range of 1.4:1 to 1.8:1. The researchers' hypothesis was that communities with a balance of jobs and housing have lower mean commute times than both communities considered job-rich and those considered job-poor. The research found that balanced communities had shorter (statistically significant) mean travel times to work than unbalanced communities.

These findings provide strong implicit evidence of possible reductions in VMT from a jobs-housing balance. One should be cognizant, however, that travel time and VMT are not the same—travel time can increase due to accidents and congestion even though distances may be shorter. Hence, the measure "mean travel time to work," as used by Weitz and Schindler (1997), is a reasonable proxy but not a perfect substitute for VMT.

Reduced tailpipe emissions and better air quality. By reducing VMT, a jobs-housing balance policy will also reduce the number of hours that vehicles are operating. A jobs-housing balance policy thus can help reduce tailpipe emissions and lead to decreases in air pollution (Armstrong and Sears 2001).

Slower increases in housing costs. The Washington Research Council (2000) has produced data showing that areas with more balanced jobs-housing growth ratios (i.e., the number of jobs added divided by the number of housing units added during a given period; see sidebar in the Applications section below) have slower increases in housing costs. The council studied the relationship between changing ratios of jobs to housing and increases in housing prices from 1990 to 1999 in three large areas of King County: South County, Westside, and Eastside. Data are shown in Table 7.

The South County area had the most balanced jobs-housing ratio of the three county subareas, with a 1.51 jobs-to-housing-unit ratio in 1999. South County was also the most balanced in terms of the 1990–1999 jobs-housing growth ratio, at 1.91. Westside and Eastside had 1999 jobs-housing ratios that are considered by most standards to be unbalanced, and their jobs-housing growth ratios were severely imbalanced, with 3.5 to 4.5 jobs added for each housing unit added between 1990 and 1999.

Westside and Eastside had 67 percent and 63 percent increases, respectively, in the average home sales prices from 1990 to 1999. The more balanced South County, by contrast, experienced an increase of 43 percent for home sale prices. Westside and Eastside also witnessed greater increases

The Washington Research Council (2000) has produced data showing that areas with more balanced jobs-housing growth ratios . . . have slower increases in housing costs.

TABLE 7
HOUSING COSTS IN RELATION TO JOBS-HOUSING RATIOS
SUBAREAS OF KING COUNTY, WASHINGTON

Characteristic	South County	Westside	Eastside
Approximate Jobs Added, 1990–1999[1]	62,000	81,000	110,000
Approximate Housing Units Added, 1990–1999[1]	33,000	18,000	31,000
Jobs-Housing Growth Ratio, 1990–1999	1.91	4.50	3.56
Jobs-Housing Ratio, 1999	1.51 (balanced)	2.04 (unbalanced)	1.85 (unbalanced)
Average House Sales Price, 1990	$134,443	$174,635	$237,161
Average House Sales Price, 1999	$192,607	$291,461	$386,918
Percentage Increase in House Sales Price, 1990–1999	43.3	66.9	63.1
Average Rent per Month) for a Two-Bedroom, One-Bath Apartment, 1990	$473	$561	$574
Average Rent per Month for a Two-Bedroom, One-Bath Apartment, 1999	$640	$858	$862
Percent Change in Average Rent for a Two-Bedroom, One-Bath Apartment, 1990–1999	35	53	50

Note: 1. Determined from a histogram; absolute numbers not provided in original source.
Source: Washington Research Council 2000

in monthly rents for apartments during the same period (53 percent and 50 percent, respectively) than South County (35 percent).

Although these findings pertain to only one county during one decade, they are robust because they are based on two measures of jobs-housing balance and two measures of housing prices. The data in Table 7 provide evidence that one area of King County with a balanced jobs-housing ratio and a more balanced job-housing growth ratio had a smaller increase in housing purchase prices and monthly rents than two unbalanced areas of the county.

While one may not be able to generalize based on these conclusions, the logic is compelling. As areas continue to add jobs, the demand increases for housing close or convenient to the jobs. When housing is not added in some reasonable proportion to jobs added, housing stock in the job-rich (unbalanced) areas becomes more scarce, and the market responds by driving up prices due to the increased demand.

Other benefits. A jobs-housing balance policy has the potential for reducing public costs of new road construction and improvements and other infrastructure costs. Jobs-housing balance policies also have more intangible benefits that match smart growth principles. Cervero (1989; 1991) suggests that balancing jobs and housing can reduce class segregation and create interesting, pedestrian-oriented places. Furthermore, jobs-housing balances reduce stress in commuting— which, in turn, can result in higher productivity—as well as contribute to greater family stability and cohesion, and provide for more diverse urban settings that exhibit cultural richness (Armstrong and Sears 2001).

Contentions That Jobs-Housing Balance Doesn't Matter

As noted by Reid Ewing (1996, 19), "detractors seem to be winning the war of words" when it comes to the concept of jobs-housing balance. Some scholars, particularly economists, are skeptical of the need for public policies that promote jobs-housing balance.

As noted by Reid Ewing, "detractors seem to be winning the war of words" when it comes to the concept of jobs-housing balance. Some scholars, particularly economists, are skeptical of the need for public policies that promote jobs-housing balance.

Economists observe that over time the "natural processes" of the market will balance jobs and housing without government intervention (Bookout 1990). Imbalances are supposedly "self-correcting" phenomena (Altshuler and Gomez-Ibanez 1993, 74–75). More jobs will gradually move into areas with a housing surplus (Downs 1992).

Critics of jobs-housing balance policies also dispute the policy assumption that workers will opt to live closer to their workplaces if given the choice. Jonathan Levine (1998) notes, for example, that households with a range of locational choices tend to seek lower residential densities at increasing distances from work. Similarly, Anthony Downs (1992) observes that numerical jobs-housing balances may still not provide housing units at costs and styles appropriate for workers. He further contends that, even if housing is available next to jobs centers where workers are employed, at appropriate prices, most of the workers will not be persuaded to live there.

Downs (1992, 99) notes further that jobs-housing imbalances "probably do contribute to traffic congestion," but he argues that even with balances "large amounts of cross-commuting would still take place" (p. 109). Downs thus casts doubt on whether altering jobs-housing imbalances will significantly reduce traffic congestion and even on whether such imbalances can be removed through public policies. Other economists, such as Terry Moore and Paul Thorsnes (1994, 81), echo these sentiments in their observation that jobs-housing balancing policies "would have little effect on travel patterns." Jonathan Levine (1998) argues that policies supporting jobs-housing balance will have little payoff in terms of reducing congestion.

Alan A. Altshuler and Jose A. Gomez-Ibanez (1993, 74), who consider the implementation of jobs-housing balancing policies to be "more of a romantic dream than a practical reality," have also found that households consider many other factors besides proximity to job sites when selecting a home. Recall the example of Kathy from the opening scenario of this report: because she wanted to buy a house but was unable to find one she could afford near her workplace, she traded a longer commute for homeownership. As Altshuler and Gomez-Ibanez (1993) indicate, Kathy's decision—affordability over proximity to work—is hardly uncommon. Other factors may be the availability of services and shopping or local school quality. For these reasons, "residents in communities planned for greater jobs-housing balance appear to commute about as far as residents of unplanned communities" (Altshuler and Gomez-Ibanez 1993, 74).

Telecommuting (or teleworking) can be viewed as one of the ultimate jobs-housing balancing tools: when one works at home, the daily commute trips are largely eliminated. In a nationwide study, Sangho Choo, Patricia L. Mokhtarian, and Ilan Salomon (2001) expressed 90 percent confidence that telecommuting reduces VMT, but they also concluded that the amount of the reduction is most likely small, falling somewhere between a 2 percent reduction and essentially no change in VMT. The authors do not explain why telecommuting does not significantly reduce VMT, but it may be safe to assume that trips other than rush-hour work trips make up the difference.

Countering the Skeptic's View

While research into the relationship between commuting and jobs-housing policies has increased during the past decade, there is still no firm consensus on the nature of that relationship. But, as indicated above, the fact that some research has clearly shown that many workers do want to live closer to their workplaces should spur planners to provide more and better opportunities for those workers. Although decreasing jobs-housing imbalances may be "extraordinarily difficult" (Downs 1992, 111), planners should not shy away from the task, especially if research continues to demonstrate that—as in King County, Washington—areas with jobs-housing balances have slower increases in housing costs than areas with imbalances.

The arguments made by critics of jobs-housing balance policies against government intervention are best evaluated within the context of the four types of imbalances described above (see Table 5 and Figure 1). As noted above, free markets are indeed the most effective at correcting jobs-housing imbalances in areas with job deficiencies (i.e., Type 4 imbalances). Private employers do not need much prodding to locate in areas with abundant and skilled labor, especially once public policies that may have forbidden employers from locating in residential areas are removed.

But what about job-deficient areas with an abundant supply of mostly unskilled labor (i.e., Type 3 imbalances)? As decades of decline in American central cities have shown, the market cannot be trusted to bring jobs to older suburban and central-city neighborhoods that house semi-skilled or unskilled labor, without government intervention. The marketplace is hardly capable on its own of correcting undersupplies of affordable housing in job-rich areas (i.e., Type 1 imbalances) either. Furthermore, the market (at least until recently) seems to have failed to produce adequate housing in the central business districts of our nation's cities (i.e., Type 2 imbalances). In the past, zoning did not allow housing downtown, and consumers may have been put off by the perception of greater crime in the central city. Government intervention in making downtown living a possibility as well as changes in the lifestyle preferences of many empty nesters and young people have contributed to a rebirth of housing (albeit not necessarily affordable housing) in many central-city downtown districts.

Three of the four jobs-housing imbalances identified in this report, therefore, can be attributed to market failure. The market seems to be able to respond in a self-correcting manner only to Type 4 imbalances, where office complexes (and also low-skilled retail and service jobs) move to serve residential areas with higher disposable incomes and more professional job skills. For instance, 80 percent of the Chicago region's new jobs are going to the region's northwestern suburbs (Benfield, Raimi, and Chen 1999). But even though the market may respond to Type 4 imbalances, the net result is not necessarily a qualitative match of jobs and housing in close proximity to one another. Some government intervention may be necessary to ensure productive growth for the region.

Yet the strongest argument against critics of jobs-housing balance policies may be workers themselves. People across the United States are growing weary of ever-longer commutes and are becoming more frustrated with traffic congestion, to the point that the job commute is beginning to weigh more heavily in decisions about where to reside. There is increasingly less of a need for planners to prove beyond a reasonable doubt that jobs-housing policies will reduce VMT and traffic congestion. We know now that many individuals and households want the choice of living closer to work; for a community to use public policy to provide that choice, therefore, is a smart political decision.

Mixed-use development may be the most promising option today for providing this choice. Planners are familiar with the concept of internal capture of vehicle trips, which can result from mixing commercial uses, such as restaurants and shops, with employment centers and housing. Mixed land uses thus provide the opportunity to reduce the number of trips and VMT. It has been shown that mixed-use development can reduce trip generation by 20 to 25 percent when compared to stand-alone, single-use development (Stover and Koepke 1988). Ewing (1996, 20) contends that "most successful new communities manage to capture upwards of a third of all work trips internally" and that "any development that helps bring

We know now that many individuals and households want the choice of living closer to work; for a community to use public policy to provide that choice, therefore, is a smart political decision.

jobs and housing into better balance within such an area should reduce average commute lengths, thereby reducing VMT." It is reasonable to suggest that a significant part of this reduction of trips in mixed-use developments can be attributed to jobs-housing balance. And even if—as many critics assert—the number of people who locate closer to work in a mixed-use development due to a jobs-housing balancing policy may be small, the shift undeniably frees up some roadway capacity that those workers would otherwise have occupied in their travel to work (Levine 1998).

All in all, implementing a jobs-housing balance policy very likely has the benefit of eliminating some commute trips, shortening some trips, and reducing overall VMT. While such reductions should not be overstated, planners should also not fall victim to critics' claims that such reductions do not exist. Planners therefore need not wait for more empirical evidence before they begin implementing jobs-housing balancing policies that provide greater choice and create potential for transportation-related benefits.

APPLICATIONS OF JOB-HOUSING BALANCING POLICIES

Jobs-housing balance policies can be applied at many different geographic levels by state, regional, county, and city governments. This section emphasizes regional applications, because the issue of balancing jobs and housing manifests itself most often in a regional context.

State Applications

California: an undisputed leader. California is an undisputed leader in jobs-housing balancing, particularly in addressing affordable housing needs in areas of rapid job growth. Since 1980, California statutes

---

CALIFORNIA DEPARTMENT OF HOUSING AND COMMUNITY DEVELOPMENT INTERREGIONAL PARTNERSHIP (IRP) GRANTS FOR JOBS-HOUSING BALANCE

Purpose	One-time allocation to be used to develop and implement plans to promote and accommodate housing development in areas rich in jobs, and job creation in predominately residential communities. Applicants are to use geographic mapping, targeted policies and incentives, and integrated planning approaches that connect housing, transportation, and environmental issues to alleviate jobs-housing imbalances
Terms	One-time funding allocation. Funded activities must be completed by June 30, 2004. Requires 25 percent local match.
Eligible Activities	Analyze effects of jobs-housing imbalances using geographic mapping; develop implementation plans, targeted policies, and incentives, and integrated planning approaches to encourage economic investment and job creation near available housing and increase housing development near major employment centers.
Eligible Applicants	Two or more councils of governments (COGs), two or more subregional agencies within a multicounty council of governments, or a county collaborating with the state and federal governments in an interregional context.

Source: California Department of Housing and Community Development (2000).

have required that each local government adopt a housing element as part of its general plan that meets state standards (Meck, Retzlaff, and Schwab 2003).

The California State Assembly Select Committee on Jobs-Housing Balance held a number of hearings into the causes of the jobs-housing imbalances across the state. The committee concluded in part that a lack of affordable housing near workplaces has contributed to traffic congestion and longer commutes (Sierra Business Council 1999).

California Assembly Bill 2864 created a multimillion dollar statewide program that uses incentives to increase housing in areas where jobs exceed housing and in areas where housing exceeds jobs (see sidebar). In 2001, for example, it provided grants for capital outlay projects to local governments aimed at increasing the number of residential building permits near jobs. A state workforce housing program is also now in place for low- and moderate-income workers, such as teachers, policemen, and clerical staff, that allows them to live in subsidized housing sites near their work (LeGates 2001).

Other states. Other states have begun to encourage or require consideration of jobs-housing balance as a land-use policy. Jobs-housing balancing is considered an alternative to urban sprawl in Florida and an option within transportation system planning in Oregon. Washington has adopted jobs-housing policies in its administrative rules (Weitz 1999), and Georgia has also implicitly incorporated the concept into its administrative rules (see sidebar).

GEORGIA DEPARTMENT OF COMMUNITY AFFAIRS: INTEGRATING JOBS-HOUSING BALANCE INTO PLANNING RULES

In December 2002, the Georgia Department of Community Affairs strengthened its minimum standards and procedures for local comprehensive planning, which will be effective January 1, 2004. The department's Office of Coordinated Planning, which is responsible for the state's coordinated planning program, prepared the rules and included a number of important planning concepts, including jobs-housing balance. As local governments in Georgia prepare new comprehensive plans, they will be required to consider these provisions, which implicitly require an analysis of the balance between jobs and housing. The following rule excerpts illustrate how the notion of jobs-housing balance has been integrated into the new planning requirements.

- "Housing Opportunities Objective: Quality housing and a range of housing size, cost, and density should be provided in each community, to make it possible for all who work in the community to also live in the community" (p.15).

- The local government must analyze "the cost of housing compared to wages and household incomes of the local government's resident and nonresident workforce" (p.27).

- For intermediate and advanced planning levels, the local government's implementation program should include programs, policies, and initiatives to "create affordable housing opportunities to insure that all those who work in the community have a viable choice or option to live in the community" (p.28).

- Such programs may include "the creation of housing within walking distance to employment and commercial centers" (p.28).

Source: Georgia Department of Community Affairs (2003).

Maryland adopted a "Live-Near-Your-Work" program in 1997, which is administered by the state's Department of Housing and Community Development. The program offers homeowners a minimum of $3,000 toward costs of purchasing homes in targeted neighborhoods near worksites. It was adopted to help reduce commuting costs and comply with federal Clean Air Act requirements (Meck, Retzlaff, and Schwab 2003).

The New England states have for some time taken leadership positions in providing affordable housing through public policies, although these are not typically touted as jobs-housing policies. Massachusetts has had a Comprehensive Permit Law since 1969 that establishes a streamlined procedure to obtain local permits to build affordable housing. Rhode Island adopted a similar statute in 1991 (Meck, Retzlaff, and Schwab 2003).

The New Jersey Fair Housing Act (1985) established the New Jersey Council on Affordable Housing that estimates needs for low- and moderate-income housing by region and allocates fair shares to each municipality in the housing region. Fair-share allocations like New Jersey's are one method that states can use to increase the supply of affordable housing in job-rich areas, if allocation formulas take job location into account. Similarly, New Hampshire requires that regional planning commissions compile regional housing needs assessments to guide municipal comprehensive planning (Meck, Retzlaff, and Schwab 2003).

Regional and Local Applications

Interregional partnership in California. The California counties of Alameda, Contra Costa, Santa Clara, San Joaquin, and Stanislaus formed an interregional partnership (IRP) to address regional issues, with improving jobs-housing balance as its top priority. Parts of this region, such as the Silicon Valley, have many more jobs than housing units, while other parts, like much of the San Joaquin Valley, have many more housing units than jobs. Furthermore, imbalances are projected to worsen over time. This IRP received funding from the state to conduct research and designate five to 10 jobs-housing opportunity sites, at least half of which were to be housing opportunity sites in areas where jobs exceed housing units (LeGates 2001).

Southern California's severe imbalances. As noted above, planning funds were made available to California governments via a jobs-housing balance improvements program initiated pursuant to Assembly Bill 2864. The Southern California Association of Governments (SCAG) prepared a detailed analysis of jobs-housing imbalances to help local governments in the SCAG region to apply for funds. These governments have been able to use SCAG's analysis to spur housing development in job-rich areas and well-paying jobs in housing-rich areas.

In the SCAG region, jobs are plentiful but housing is scarce, and prices and rents have soared. There is a lack of housing construction near major jobs centers, and many workers cannot afford to purchase what little housing is being produced. Job-rich areas are located primarily in southern Los Angeles County and northern Orange County, while housing-rich areas are located on the periphery of the region, especially in the Inland Empire area and in northern Los Angeles County. Although some job growth has occurred and is expected to continue in the Inland Empire and northern Los Angeles County, these new jobs are primarily in low-paying, blue-collar sectors of the economy. Average wages are insufficient to purchase the average local house in the Inland Empire. The result is that service and blue-collar workers are forced to commute long distances from areas where they can find affordable homes.

Confounding problems is SCAG's finding that there is an insufficient amount of raw, developable land in Los Angeles and Orange Counties to accommodate forecasted needs. Some counties have excess vacant land zoned for commercial and industrial uses, and the SCAG report cites the

Fair-share allocations like New Jersey's are one method that states can use to increase the supply of affordable housing in job-rich areas, if allocation formulas take job location into account.

fiscalization of land use as a primary cause of regional jobs-housing imbalances. Because of property tax limitations, local governments are overzoning for nonresidential development and not providing sufficient residential development. Gentrification can also occur near nodes of high technology development, as affluent workers displace low- and moderate-income groups in the limited housing supplies around the nodes.

SCAG planners used 55 Regional Statistical Areas (compilations of census tracts) derived from SCAG's regional transportation plan as their primary unit of analysis. The 1997 regional average ratio of jobs to households was 1.25 jobs per household, defined as an occupied housing unit. According to research done by SCAG planners, there is little public support for commuting more than 30 minutes. Consequently, SCAG used an average commute speed in the region of about 28 mph to calculate that commutesheds have radii of about 14 miles around employment centers.

SCAG's report analyzes jobs-housing imbalance conditions in terms of current land-use patterns as well as forecasted land-use patterns by regional statistical area. It finds, for example, that almost all of Orange County is projected to be job-rich by 2025. Orange County is not adding enough housing to house all of the county's workers or to keep up with job production, and, as a result, its jobs-housing imbalance will worsen in the next 20 years. More and more workers will need to commute to Orange County from other areas of the region, primarily from the Inland Empire. The report concludes that aggressive and substantial infill housing development policies are needed in Los Angeles and Orange Counties and other job-rich areas of the region. Well-paying jobs are needed in the Inland Empire. Other housing strategies suggested by the report include transit-oriented development and revisions to zoning ordinances.

Region 2040: Alternative growth concepts in the Portland region. The well-known Portland, Oregon, Region 2040 study evaluates jobs-housing impacts on a regional and subregional basis as part of a long-range growth management process. Using a computerized spatial allocation model, Metro's planners developed and analyzed three growth concepts in addition to a base case. Their analysis included many factors, such as air-quality impacts and transportation costs, but this section focuses solely on the report's findings about jobs-housing balance.

The Portland region as of the mid-1990s had a balance of jobs and housing, but many subareas of the region were unbalanced. Each of the growth concepts presented in the study—Concepts A, B, and C—was found to have different impacts on jobs-housing balance.

Public participation exercises were also held as a part of Region 2040. Interviewers asked residents about their preferred locations for living and working. Table 8 provides the various results. Residents do not show an

Orange County is not adding enough housing to house all of the county's workers or to keep up with job production, and, as a result, its jobs-housing imbalance will worsen in the next 20 years.

TABLE 8
PREFERENCES FOR LIVING/WORKING BY LOCATION
PORTLAND METRO REGION 2040 SURVEY RESULTS
(Percentages of Total Respondents)

Source	Percentage Favor Living/Working in Same Area	Percentage Favor Living/Working Both Same Area and Separate Areas	Percentage Favor Living/Working in Separate Areas
Random telephone survey (n = 397)	27	42	30
Stakeholder interviews (n = 53)	49	35	16
Local government survey (n = 83)	43	38	19
Public workshops (n = 64)	50	34	16

Note: Figures may not add up to 100% due to rounding.
Source: Metro (1994a, Figures 2.1–2.4).

overwhelming preference for being able to work and live in the same area, perhaps reflecting existing subarea imbalances and a tendency for residents to favor the status quo. On the other hand, the results show that a plurality of respondents to a random phone survey favored the choice of living and working in the same or separate areas. These findings thus underscore the assertion made above that it is important that residents are provided better choices of living and working areas and that some have a preference for living closer to their jobs (Metro 1994a).

Table 9 summarizes data for the base case—in which existing trends were simply extrapolated—and the three growth concepts. The base case and Concepts A and B are quite similar in terms of the total jobs and households in the region. Concept C results in less growth in the region but still has a reasonably comparable jobs-housing balance. The fact that jobs and household numbers are comparable allows one to isolate the effects of differences in urban form.

TABLE 9
IMPACTS OF GROWTH CONCEPTS
ON JOBS-HOUSEHOLDS BALANCE
METRO'S REGION 2040

Description	Base Case: Existing trends continued	Concept A: Some expansion of urban growth boundary (UGB)	Concept B: No expansion of UGB	Concept C: One-third of new growth channeled to satellite cities
Jobs	1,284,210	1,305,193	1,293,427	1,169,913
Households	827,843	839,333	822,452	724,836
Jobs + Housing	2,112,053	2,144,526	2,115,879	1,894,749
Jobs-Household Ratio	1.55:1	1.55:1	1.57:1	1.61:1
Percent of growth in existing Metro UGB	83	71	100	63
Vehicle miles traveled per capita	13.4	12.48	10.86	11.92

Source: Metro 1994b, Figure 5. Ratios calculated by author.

Concept B, which would (a) provide for compact development with no increase in the UGB, (b) add only a few road improvements, and (c) change zoning toward mixed uses, was found to do the most for achieving regional jobs-housing balance.

Concept A, which would expand the urban growth boundary (UGB), resulted in jobs-housing imbalances in the UGB expansion areas (largely residential areas), while certain central commercial areas in the region favored jobs over housing in the buildout concept. Some balanced sub-regions did exist in Concept A.

Concept B, which would (a) provide for compact development with no increase in the UGB, (b) add only a few road improvements, and (c) change zoning toward mixed uses, was found to do the most for achieving regional jobs-housing balance. Concept B would minimize imbalances in two ways: by not adding residential land at the periphery, and by creating more mixed uses throughout the region. There would still be imbalances at the subregional level, while other parts such as those outside Portland's central business district would be balanced in terms of jobs and households.

Concept C, which would allow minor UGB expansion and allocate one-third of future growth to satellite cities, would provide for balances of jobs and households within those satellite cities. VMT would exceed that in Concept B due to traffic between the Metro area and the satellite cities, but it would be less than that in Concept A due to the mix of jobs and housing that would occur throughout the region. Jobs-housing imbalances would occur within the minor UGB expansions, and several subregional areas would also be imbalanced (Metro 1994a).

The lessons of Region 2040 with regard to jobs-housing balancing policies are many. The report demonstrates that, when considering growth concepts and future development scenarios, planners should strive to achieve a balance of jobs and housing at both regional and subregional levels. Mixed land uses can help achieve better balances. But Region 2040 also shows that some areas of the region will remain unbalanced because even major efforts to change land use are unlikely to balance jobs and housing in what are now predominantly residential areas or job-rich city centers. Importantly, the predicted effect of Metro's analysis of the growth concepts is that more concentrated and mixed uses will result in reduced VMT and, consistent with the stated preferences of citizens in the region, will allow residents greater freedom in choosing where they want to live and work.

Longmont, Colorado: A model for other cities in the Denver region. As a part of its Metro 2030 plan, the Denver Regional Council of Governments met with city leaders to see if they could fashion and implement jobs-housing balancing strategies that would shorten commutes in the region. Longmont, which is a 40-minute drive north of Denver, has implemented a jobs-housing balance that has attracted "a mix of high-tech companies and smaller businesses that match with the skills of the people who live there" (Siebert 2003). Whereas regionally only 36 percent of the people who work in a local community live there, in Longmont 80 percent of the people who work there live there, according to a 1997 study by the Denver COG.

According to John Cody, president of the Longmont Area Economic Council, city leaders pushed to balance housing with jobs because "they didn't want to be a bedroom community anymore" (Siebert 2003). Longmont has achieved that balance by working with developers and by making it easier for high-technology firms and small businesses to locate in the city.

Planners and policy makers are realistic about their expectations: they don't assume jobs-housing balance will immediately eliminate traffic congestion, but they do view jobs-housing balancing policies as one of a limited number of options.

A jobs-to-population ratio in the Boulder Valley, Colorado. Boulder Valley has witnessed jobs-population imbalances since at least the early 1990s. Several efforts have materialized to reduce projected job growth in certain areas, including a nonresidential growth management system and, in 1997, a comprehensive rezoning of the city of Boulder's downtown and industrial areas that converted some land to residential uses and reduced intensities. The former was problematic, but the latter was successful at reducing projected job growth by more than 11,000 jobs (City of Boulder n.d.).

As a part of a major update to the Boulder Valley Comprehensive Plan in August 2001, the city of Boulder and Boulder County adopted an initial jobs-to-population balancing policy (see sidebar). The ratio of jobs to population in Boulder Valley was 0.92 to 1 (107,074 jobs to 114,580 population) in the year 2000 and was projected to increase to 1.21 to 1 by the year 2020. Implementation of the policy began in October 2001 with appointment of a jobs-population balance task force. Through its transportation planning process, the city and county developed and calibrated a transportation model that included three jobs-housing scenarios (City of Boulder n.d.).

GETTING STARTED: SOME RECOMMENDED STEPS

This section provides a step-by-step method for considering and applying jobs-housing balance in a local comprehensive plan and land-use regulations. More specific considerations for comprehensive plans and land-use regulations are provided in subsequent sections of this report.

Step 1. Determine the appropriate unit of geography for the study and application of jobs-housing balance policies. There is no accepted geographic scale within which to assess the match or mismatch of jobs and housing (Levine 1998). Ewing (1996) recommends considering jobs-hous-

JOBS-TO-POPULATION BALANCE POLICY IN BOULDER VALLEY

The generally accepted planning standard for a balanced jobs-to-population ratio is 0.65 to 1. Given current policies, the city and county agree that the current ratio within the Boulder Valley exceeds an appropriate ratio and the planning standard, and that a worsening of that ratio beyond 1:1 will lead to greater regional traffic congestion, affordable housing shortfalls, and other negative impacts on the community as a whole. The city will therefore embark on a public process to determine whether or not the 1:1 ratio is appropriate. This will be accomplished through a public process that will establish an appropriate and acceptable jobs-to-population ratio and identify a combination of actions that will reduce the amount of commercial growth, create more affordable housing, and mitigate the impacts of traffic congestion (City of Boulder n.d., B-2–B-3).

ing balance within a three- to five-mile radius of any given location of interest. Jobs-housing balance policies, however, can apply to many geographic areas depending on local needs. Policies that seek to mix land uses to achieve a jobs-housing balance can apply to individual buildings, single development sites, planned unit developments, individual neighborhoods, or subareas of the jurisdiction. Jobs-housing balancing policies can also apply citywide, countywide, or regionally. Local governments may choose one or more of these units of geography for analysis and application, but they should first prepare a broad—citywide or countywide—estimate of jobs-housing balance, which will provide initial data and insights about whether other geographic units of analysis should be used.

Step 2. Determine what jobs-housing measurement will be used, according to the available or obtainable data. There are many options for quantitatively measuring jobs-housing balance in a community or study area. No single operational definition of jobs-housing balance is widely accepted today, although the jobs-to-housing-unit ratio appears to be used most commonly.

The manner in which one defines jobs-housing balance and calculates jobs-housing ratios depends on the data available. Because there are many possible measures of jobs-housing balance, let data availability guide your choice. In Georgia, for example, the number of jobs for larger cities and all counties are reported on an annual basis by the Georgia Department of Labor. The U.S. Bureau of Census reports the number of housing units in a city or county decennially. A council of governments may provide annual estimates of the total number of housing units. Housing unit estimates are provided by the U.S. Bureau of Census and can also be derived from data on new housing starts as reported to the U.S. Bureau of Census by the local building official. Likewise, city and county general plans include some estimates of total housing units. For smaller subareas of a jurisdiction, data may be available by traffic analysis zones (TAZs) if a local government has developed a model-based transportation plan.

Jobs-housing balancing measures might include the following:

- Jobs-to-housing-units ratio

- Jobs-to-occupied-housing-units ratio

- Percentage of workers who reside locally

- Employment-to-population ratio

- Jobs-to-resident-workers (labor force) ratio

Which measurement is best? The goal of a jobs-housing balance policy is usually to match the number of working opportunities (jobs) with the number of living opportunities (housing units) in a given area. Thus the number of resident workers—the actual labor force—is the best measure to use, if available. Any other measures used to estimate the number of working opportunities in an area must be used with some caution. If, for example, a community relies on the number of housing units or households to represent demand for working opportunities in a measure of jobs-housing balance, that measure may inaccurately represent the actual number of workers living in a community: one housing unit or household may consist of any number of workers, or it may consist of no workers. Despite its potential shortcomings, however, the jobs-to-housing-unit ratio is the most common measure of jobs-housing balance, and it is certainly an adequate measure so long as the applied jobs-housing balance standard is adjusted to account for the average number of workers per housing unit in the region or locality.

No single operational definition of jobs-housing balance is widely accepted today, although the jobs-to-housing-unit ratio appears to be used most commonly.

Step 3. Collect data on the jobs-housing measure you select for the study area or areas. Calculate the overall jobs-housing ratio (or whichever measure you choose) for the area and analyze the results of the calculation. The labor force in a given city or county is the number of residents in that city or county who are working or seeking work. Employment data are reported on the basis of a worker's place of work; that is, the data describe the number of occupied working positions—the number of people who work in that particular community. The occupants of those jobs may or may not reside in the same jurisdiction in which the job is located. Employment figures are typically available in city and county general plans, or they are reported annually by state labor departments (usually for individual counties but not cities).

With these data in hand, calculating an area's employment-to-labor force ratio is straightforward. This ratio should always be calculated using statistics from the same year. If annual data are not available, extrapolation methods should be used to estimate the given year for which measurements are being made.

Once you complete these calculations, look at the result and determine what it means. Are there more jobs than housing units (or labor force participants)? Are there fewer jobs than housing units (or labor force participants)? What are the implications of this difference for your community?

Step 4. Make a value judgment—select a standard and recommend/seek approval of a jobs-housing balance standard. The hardest part of pursuing a jobs-housing balance policy is determining what the policy will be. As noted above, policy making needs to be done after planners, with much public input, make their recommendations, and after local elected officials make several important decisions. Note that even the decision on how to define jobs-housing balance (Step 2) and the area to which the measurement applies (Step 1) might be considered policy decisions in and of themselves. If they are, it is desirable to present various alternatives to decision makers if data allow.

What jobs-housing standard should be used? This, again, is a local policy decision, and the answer depends on the measure used. The jobs-housing literature, however, provides guidance. As noted previously, a jobs-to-housing-units ratio of 1.5 : 1 implies balance if the average number of workers per household is 1.5. Note that the average number of workers per household can vary from community to community, and the standard should be based on an analysis of local data on workers per household. Scholars often recommend a range to signify balance, such as 1.3 : 1 to 1.7 : 1 (Ewing 1996) or 1.4 : 1 to 1.6 : 1 (Cervero 1991). If a jobs-to-employed-residents ratio is selected, a target standard of 1 : 1 implies balance and a target range of 0.8 : 1 to 1.25 : 1 is recommended (Cervero 1996). If communities try to match working residents (labor force) with employment in the community, then a one-to-one (1 : 1) relationship is the ideal.

Step 5. Audit your locality's comprehensive plan to determine the extent to which it promotes your new jobs-housing goal. Once you know whether you have a jobs-housing balance or imbalance, and you have established a jobs-housing goal, a logical next step is to review the housing, economic development, and land-use elements of the comprehensive plan to see if they promote or hinder a jobs-housing balance. For instance, the jobs-housing ratio you applied, and the standard your community selected (Step 4), should tell you whether you need more houses or more jobs in the community to obtain a balance. These measures can also tell you how much of each to provide given local growth conditions. Review housing unit projections to see if they provide the desired numbers. Check the employment

Scholars often recommend a range to signify balance, such as 1.3 : 1 to 1.7 : 1 (Ewing 1996) or 1.4 : 1 to 1.6 : 1 (Cervero 1991).

projections and economic development policies to see if they are working in tandem with your jobs-housing balancing goal. If not, they will need to be changed. You should also review the acreage figures and other aspects of the land-use element. Does the land-use plan provide for the amount of land needed to produce the desired number of houses (or jobs)? An answer to this question will require detailed analyses of land supply and development buildout.

Note that the audit should also consider qualitative balancing factors as well. For instance, will the types of housing units in the future be of the right price, location, and quality to meet the local labor force needs? Data on the types of housing units and their costs and on the types of jobs available should help you to consider not just a numerical match of jobs and housing but a qualitative balance as well. These data can sometimes be found in the local comprehensive plans of communities with detailed housing and economic development elements.

Step 6. Amend your comprehensive plan to include the analysis of jobs-housing balance and to include policy statements appropriate to your locality. Jobs-housing policies, and the data that support them, should be included in the comprehensive plan. The jobs-housing goal selected should be specified in relevant places of the comprehensive plan: the housing, economic development, and land-use elements. The degree to which the local comprehensive plan needs to be amended will depend on how well these elements already support the jobs-housing balance goal. Major revisions may be required—indeed, it is possible that the land-use plan does not support the jobs-housing balance goal at all, in which case a major revision of the land-use plan would be required. Data on existing jobs-housing ratios is best inserted in the land-use element, since that is where the decision on how to balance jobs and housing come together in the form of a recommendation for future land use. Further considerations about jobs-housing balancing policies in relation to your comprehensive plan are provided in the following section.

Step 7. Prepare and adopt regulations that implement local jobs-housing balance policies. There are a number of alternatives available to local governments that want to amend their land-use regulations to provide for greater balances of jobs and housing. Suggested considerations are provided in a subsequent section of this report.

ADOPTING JOBS-HOUSING BALANCE POLICIES IN COMPREHENSIVE PLANS
This section and those that follow supplement the general step-by-step approach described in the prior section.

Understanding the Role of the Comprehensive Plan
Most local governments have adopted a comprehensive plan that includes a future land-use plan or map. The future land-use plan establishes a community's vision that translates needs for new jobs and new housing units into a recommended pattern, mix, and intensity of land uses. Future land-use plans tell citizens, developers, and local decision makers the approximate locations in the community where houses should be built and employment centers should be established. These plans, therefore, should be closely linked to the need for future development as determined by projections of population and employment growth.

A local government's land-use plan should guide development in a way that all community goals are realized. These goals may include a high quality of life, good housing opportunities, and jobs close to home that pay suitable wages, all of which can be achieved through policies that promote jobs-housing balance.

It is possible that the land-use plan does not support the jobs-housing balance goal at all, in which case a major revision of the land-use plan would be required.

Providing Data to Inform Decision Makers

Local governments must have some knowledge of existing conditions before they can consider what changes need to be made. Local planners may find themselves unprepared to answer questions about what the current jobs-housing balance is in their community. One needs to analyze local conditions closely before policy decisions about jobs-housing balance can be made. Planners should begin by collecting data on existing employment and housing in the locality.

Prior to making policy choices about jobs-housing balances (or determining what to do about imbalances), planners should analyze the comprehensive plan to determine existing policies about the balance of jobs and housing. Community planners need to conduct a review or audit of the comprehensive plan, and chances are they will find that the local comprehensive plan does not directly address the issue of balancing jobs and housing. A community may find that additional data are needed to compute jobs-housing ratios or to address other jobs-housing balancing policy questions. For methods on how to audit your comprehensive plan with regard to jobs-housing balance, see Weitz and Waldner (2002).

An updated comprehensive plan with existing and projected population, housing, and employment data is absolutely essential to the implementation of a jobs-housing policy. Communities that wish to go beyond a basic quantitative evaluation of jobs-housing balance to consider qualitative balance will need more refined data on the types of jobs and housing needs in the community. Data should include measures of employment by occupation or industry as well as of housing type, affordability, and whatever other information may be available, such as amenities. Extensive data on the locations of employment centers and housing are also essential. If the data needed to compute jobs-housing ratios are not in the comprehensive plan now, they will need to be collected and preferably adopted as a part of the plan. For more information on collecting data that will allow qualitative assessments of how well jobs match local needs, see the method presented in the section on large-scale development below.

Setting Goals and Choosing Policies

Through the comprehensive planning process, community leaders must decide if they want to pursue a jobs-housing balance policy. Arriving at that conclusion, however, may be far easier than deciding what policy will best achieve that goal. Should the policy be to add more employment centers or more residential subdivisions, or both? The answers are often intertwined with competing community objectives. Achieving a consensus on exactly what type of policy a community will pursue can be time consuming. Efforts to set goals, build consensus, and decide on policy are best achieved through the public participation processes of a comprehensive planning exercise.

It is up to local government leaders and citizens, with assistance from planners, to decide the mix of jobs, housing, and other land uses that they want in their community now and in the future. Establishing a specific ratio within this mix may be a point of strong contention. Some communities consider alternative development scenarios and decide they want to be, or remain, a bedroom community, and so they prepare land-use plans that encourage more houses than jobs. Other communities might aggressively pursue commercial and industrial development and thus strive to be a shopping or employment center, with many more jobs than houses. Still others might, for reasons stated in this report, seek to balance jobs and housing in their communities.

Communities that wish to go beyond a basic quantitative evaluation of jobs-housing balance to consider qualitative balance will need more refined data on the types of jobs and housing needs in the community.

For those local governments that do not have a goal of obtaining a general balance between jobs and housing, it is becoming more important to consider the implications of not providing such a balance. Sometimes intentionally, but more often unintentionally, local land-use plans and zoning regulations result in land-use patterns that guide housing developments into areas far removed from workplaces. The cumulative impact of these local decisions can be substantial. When many communities in a given region have land-use plans that result in spatial mismatches between jobs and housing, traffic gridlock on a regional scale often results.

The comprehensive plan text should incorporate any written analyses of jobs-housing ratios, and it should state whether the community has adopted a jobs-housing balance policy. Hence, the comprehensive plan should serve as the "home" for any adopted jobs-housing policy.

BENCHMARKING FOR JOBS-HOUSING BALANCE: THE JOBS-HOUSING GROWTH RATIO

Most jobs-housing balancing programs look at one simple measure of jobs-housing balance at a given point in time (i.e., a cross-sectional approach), such as a jobs-to-households or jobs-to-housing unit ratio. The Washington Research Council (2000) has employed another benchmark—a jobs to housing growth ratio (i.e., a longitudinal approach), which measures the number of jobs added in relation to the number of housing units added for a given time period (also see Table 7 of this report). While the cross-sectional jobs-housing ratio remains an important statistic to consider, planners can determine the extent to which more recent development is adding to the balance or further worsening the imbalance of jobs and housing. For instance, a jobs center may have historically unbalanced jobs-housing ratios, but progress in terms of mitigating unbalanced conditions (through infill housing policies, for example) can be measured over time using the jobs-housing growth ratio.

Ensuring Policy Consistency

The comprehensive plan should not only include a specific policy intended to balance jobs and housing; all elements of the comprehensive plan should also work together to achieve that policy. Your community may have adopted the goal of being able to live and work within the community, but your adopted land-use plan and zoning regulations may actually work against that objective. If, for example, you recently changed your land-use plan to make your community a bedroom community dominated by single-family houses, long-time lower-income residents may be forced to relocate if affordable housing options disappear. Recent high school or college graduates, schoolteachers, or other service-sector employees will likely find it difficult to remain in a community if only large, single-family homes are available.

Local planners and decision makers must ensure that if their community's plan expresses job-housing balance as a goal, parts of the comprehensive plan (and local zoning regulations) do not contradict that goal. It is most important to clearly identify policies in the land-use element, but it is also important to ensure that the housing element and economic development element work in tandem with a land-use policy to encourage or require jobs-housing balance. Otherwise, the housing or economic development element may be internally inconsistent with the land-use policy, which would render the policy meaningless. The land-use, housing, and economic development elements of the comprehensive plan must be integrated to be effective.

INTEGRATING JOBS-HOUSING BALANCE INTO LAND-USE REGULATIONS

Communities are built in a mostly piecemeal fashion. Even if a city or county has a carefully considered land-use plan, it has limited control over how the community fabric is woven together. Local governments make decisions on whether to approve individual development proposals after considering the recommendations of their land-use plans and the needs of the community. Local zoning and other land-use regulations control the location of development, but they provide virtually no control over development timing (i.e., when certain parts of the community are built). As a result, development often takes place on a lot-by-lot or "incremental" basis. This uneven development may mean that even the best comprehensive plans may not be implemented due to circumstances beyond the local government's control, such as market conditions and developers' decisions on development timing and mix.

Local governments, however, need to minimize the ways in which their regulations encourage incremental development so as to minimize its negative impacts on achieving a balance between jobs and housing. Barriers or obstacles to jobs-housing-balanced development practices may need to be removed from local land-use regulations. Many zoning ordinances act as impediments to achieving jobs-housing balance policies.

In many instances, local governments should change zoning regulations to allow mixes of land uses that will bring better balance between jobs and housing. They should also work to ensure that jobs and housing are developed simultaneously. There are a wide variety of techniques that directly or indirectly support jobs-housing balancing policies and objectives. There are also a number of specific ways that local governments can change their land-use regulations to provide for jobs-housing balance, as described further in this section.

Provide For Mixed Land Uses

Where appropriate, developments can and should provide different land uses (i.e., both residences and employment) to provide the potential for opportunities to live and work in proximity. Planners should consider amending use provisions of zoning districts to allow mixed uses. For instance, many local zoning regulations still do not allow any type of residence in commercial districts, but a second-story residential unit above a ground floor of office or commercial space can be a convenient and appropriate use in downtown areas. Local governments should review the per-

Barriers or obstacles to jobs-housing-balanced development practices may need to be removed from local land-use regulations. Many zoning ordinances act as impediments to achieving jobs-housing balance policies.

mitted uses provisions of all zoning districts and amend them in cases where it is appropriate to mix residential, office, commercial, and institutional uses in the same zone and on the same parcel of land.

Consider Revisions to the Zoning Map that Will Bring Jobs Closer to Neighborhoods

Rigid separation of land uses in neighborhoods runs counter to jobs-housing balance objectives. The land-use plan and zoning ordinance should be revised to provide for neighborhood commercial centers or the establishment of employment areas in appropriate locations to meet the jobs-housing balance policies. Planners should consider allowing a corner store or neighborhood commercial zone at the edge of neighborhoods. In areas of a city or town that are almost exclusively residential neighborhoods, small-scale convenience centers at the edge of exclusively residential subdivisions can offer employment opportunities for nearby residents. (See Figure 2.) The proximity of neighborhood commercial uses can also shorten certain vehicle trips and eliminate some trips altogether if close enough for employees and patrons to reach by foot or bicycle.

Require or Encourage Planned Unit Developments (PUDs) To Provide a Mix of Residences and Employment that Promotes Jobs-Housing Balance

Planned unit developments (PUDs) are often viewed as a way to mix different types of housing with nonresidential uses on the same site or as part of the same subarea. PUDs are a type of development that allows mixtures of housing types with some supportive neighborhood commercial uses. PUDs are significant growth management strategies because they enable the community to manage the timing and sequencing of development (Weitz 2003).

Planners in localities that have already adopted a PUD ordinance should review the mixtures of land uses that are mandated or encouraged. The PUD ordinance might need to be revised to provide for a better balance of jobs and housing units. For example, PUD regulations might specify that 10 percent of the housing units be live/work units, or that the minimum percentage of developed land devoted to civic, office, and neighborhood commercial space be from 10 to 25 percent of the total site area. PUD regulations should also include a purpose statement that expresses the goal of a balance between jobs and housing.

Planners should, however, give careful thought to what minimum size is needed for a PUD to ensure the land-use mix the community desires. As the author has elsewhere observed,

> A certain critical mass or economic threshold is needed to create the demand for certain activities that are sometimes part of PUDs. According to DeChiara, Panero, and Zelnick (1995), a population of 500 will support activities such as a day-care center, church, playground, and a corner store. A PUD with 200 homes (assuming 2.5 persons per home) would be large enough to support such activities. The minimum size of a PUD needed to support these activities would depend on the density permitted. If the PUD's density averages five units per acre, the minimum parcel size of a PUD to support these other activities is 40 acres. At a more suburban density of three units per acre, the minimum size to meet the threshold for other specified activities is more than 65 acres. (Weitz 2003)

A PUD that is too small to support commercial activities, therefore, risks intensifying an existing jobs-housing imbalance.

Promote Jobs-Housing Balance Through Home Occupation Regulations

Local governments should review the strictness of their home occupation regulations and liberalize them to allow a broader range of home-work

A certain critical mass or economic threshold is needed to create the demand for certain activities that are sometimes part of PUDs.

arrangements while maintaining the character of a residential neighborhood. A home occupation, where a worker conducts business in the home, is the "ultimate" in jobs-housing balance, both qualitatively and quantitatively. Review existing local home occupation regulations to see if they unduly restrict living and working in the same dwelling unit, provided that the home occupations to be allowed are consistent with maintaining peace and quiet in residential neighborhoods. You may also want to revise home occupation regulations to encourage teleworking. For more information, see Wunder (2000).

Permit Accessory Units or "Garage Apartments"

Accessory units are small units added to existing single-family homes that offer a low-cost apartment for single persons. As a strategy, providing for accessory units can be an efficient housing remedy in places with an abundance of jobs or college students and low-density, single-family neighborhoods. It is often more acceptable to the citizenry to preserve the existing character of the neighborhood by allowing accessory units instead of encouraging large apartment complexes.

Permit Live/Work Units

Unlike a home occupation, in which a resident works in a dwelling, a live/work unit is a housing unit specifically designed to be both a residence and a work place for the occupant of the unit. But like a home occupation, a live/work unit is another ultimate in jobs-housing balance. Zoning ordinances can be amended to provide for live/work units in certain zoning districts, as appropriate. Live/work units are often a permitted use in areas governed by traditional neighborhood development (TND) regulations.

A home occupation, where a worker conducts business in the home, is the "ultimate" in jobs-housing balance, both qualitatively and quantitatively.

SELECTED INCENTIVE PROGRAMS FOR INCREASING HOUSING OPPORTUNITIES

Housing Opportunity Incentive	Description and Application
Closing bonuses	Maryland offers a $3,000 closing bonus to people who buy homes in established neighborhoods close to their jobs.
Location-efficient mortgages	Available to households locating close to public transit; a pilot program sponsored by the Federal National Mortgage Association and the National Resources Defense Council is in place in the Bay Area.
Streamlined housing permitting	One-stop or other expedited permitting processes to reduce the length of time it takes to get permits. Operational in many Inter-Regional Partnership (IRP) area jurisdictions.
Minimum density requirements	Regulations that establish minimum residential densities for new housing near transit stations. A popular alternative with many jurisdictions already implementing this tool.
Employer assisted housing	Employers subsidize housing for their workers. A few institutions in the IRP area have implemented this tool.
Housing impact or "linkage" fees	Fees on new commercial and industrial projects to generate funds for affordable housing. In place in several IRP jurisdictions, and several are willing to consider such fees.

Source: LeGates (2001).

Inclusionary Zoning

Inclusionary housing programs require developers and builders to include affordable housing in market-rate housing developments (Porter 1997). The Montgomery County, Maryland, inclusionary housing program has been described elsewhere (White 1992) and does not require reiteration here. Rockville, Maryland, Anaheim, California, and Aspen and Breckenridge, Colorado, have also adopted inclusionary zoning ordinances (Porter 1997). Other localities with mandatory inclusionary zoning programs include Boulder, Colorado, Davis, California, and Pitkin County, Colorado. Voluntary inclusionary housing programs also exist in Dallas, Texas, Hilton Head, South Carolina, and Orlando, Florida (White 1992). Inclusionary zoning is most appropriate in mitigating Type 1 jobs-housing imbalances.

Linkage Programs

A specific technique for implementing a jobs-housing balance policy on a local level is a mandatory linkage program. A linkage policy requires major employers to secure or provide housing for a portion of any new workforce created by those employers (usually, for low- and moderate-income households). Linkage policies are one way to implement a jobs-housing objective of ensuring that new, affordable housing units are constructed and are accessible to new workplaces. Hence, they are most appropriate for application in Type 1 jobs-housing imbalances.

Jurisdictions in California, Massachusetts, and New Jersey have adopted mandatory linkage programs, with San Francisco, Berkeley, and Boston cited as some of the leading local examples (Altshuler and Gomez-Ibanez 1993). These programs are not legal everywhere, however. For local governments in states that may not provide a solid legal footing for a mandatory linkage program, a voluntary program may be appropriate. There are at least three local voluntary linkage programs in Florida and at least one locality with a voluntary linkage program in Connecticut, New Jersey, and Washington (Altshuler and Gomez-Ibanez 1993).

Incentives

Another variation to address Type 1 imbalances is a density bonus. Bellevue, Washington, has a density bonus program that allows developers to build four additional square feet of office space for every square foot of housing provided (Cervero 1991). Some communities also use reduced fees and streamlined permit processes to stimulate development that will correct jobs-housing imbalances. Local governments might reward subdivision or apartment developers with various incentives (e.g., density increases, expedited processing times, development impact fee waivers) if developers ensure that a certain minimum percentage of housing units constructed will be affordable to low- and moderate-income households.

ENSURING QUALITATIVE BALANCE IN LARGE-SCALE DEVELOPMENT REVIEWS

This section describes a method and data sources that allow analysis of the qualitative balancing of jobs and housing in large-scale developments. It is based on work by Jerry Weitz & Associates, Inc. for the Georgia Regional Transportation Authority's Development of Regional Impact Program. (For a background summary of that work, see sidebar.)

The Rationale for Area of Influence (AOI) Analyses

Since 2002, the Georgia Regional Transportation Authority has regulated developments it believes are "likely to have an impact beyond the host local government's jurisdiction" (GRTA 2003 [http://www.georgiaplanning.com/planners/dri/history.htm]). These large-

A specific technique for implementing a jobs-housing balance policy on a local level is a mandatory linkage program.

Since the inception of the Georgia Planning Act of 1989, the Georgia Department of Community Affairs (DCA) has adminstered a development of regional impact (DRI) program. Administrative rules of DCA require that developments meeting certain minimum thresholds (e.g., 400 residential lots, depending on the region of the state) must undergo a review process by the regional planning agency with regard to regional impacts. DCA's program of DRIs has historically had little enforcement power, and some local governments (to the admonishment of DCA) have not complied with the letter of the program requirements.

The DRI program took on additional significance, however, within the 13-county nonattainment area of Atlanta when in 2002 the Georgia Regional Transportation Authority adopted administrative rules, *Procedures and Principles for GRTA Development of Regional Impact (DRI) Review*. GRTA has legislative responsibilities to review DRI applications for land use, transportation, and air-quality impacts. GRTA's rules, which are in addition to DCA's, specify a rigorous set of transportation modeling requirements for DRIs. In addition, there are provisions that require a DRI applicant to study the project's impact in relationship to development in its "Area of Influence" (AOI), or an area extending six road miles from the development in all directions. The DRI rules are complex, and the AOI requirements require elaborate investigations of jobs-housing qualitative relationships.

To aid in the preparation and administration of DRI applications relative to AOIs, GRTA sponsored the preparation of guidebooks for GRTA in order to provide simple methods and to identify and evaluate data sources for AOI analyses. These GRTA guidebooks have been used to describe some of these methods in this PAS Report.

scale developments—called developments of regional impact, or DRIs—are defined by GTRA as those developments that meet certain thresholds for development type. These developments typically include a range of residential and commercial uses. GTRA has determined that the area most heavily impacted by a DRI is that within six miles of it, which is called the DRI's area of influence (AOI). Perhaps the most important element of the AOI is its transportation system; the efficiency of local roads and highways are likely to be determined by the jobs-housing mix in the DRI.

If a DRI is job-poor, its residents will likely overburden the transportation system commuting to jobs in or beyond the AOI, resulting in long commutes. When a DRI includes nonresidential uses (e.g., offices, retail commercial, etc.), however, it creates employment opportunities. Residents in the DRI may be able to find work within the DRI, but only if the types of jobs available there match the types of housing available: lower-wage workers, for example, will only be able to live and work in the DRI if affordable housing and lower-wage jobs are created. If workers cannot find appropriate and affordable housing within the DRI (or AOI), they will have to travel longer distances between the DRI and their residences. As a result, regional vehicle miles traveled (VMT) will increase. So too, commuting times will increase across the region.

One of GRTA's goals is to increase the mix of land uses in DRIs so that VMT will be reduced. Large-scale developments should have land-use mixes that encourage shorter vehicle trips, in terms of both distance and time. In short, the GRTA's DRI regulations aim to make it possible for workers who fill jobs in the DRI to live in the DRI and the AOI.

GRTA'S AOI STANDARDS

GRTA requires three different jobs-housing balancing benchmarks, which are listed below. GRTA evaluates proposed DRIs to determine the extent to which they satisfy these criteria. Approval of a DRI's plan of development is dependent on meeting one of these criteria. The wording is taken directly from Procedures and Principles for GTRA Development of Regional Impact Review (GTRA 2002), which requires that the DRI:

- contains a mix of uses that are reasonably anticipated to contribute to a balancing of land uses such that it would be affordable for at least 10 percent of the persons who are reasonably anticipated to be employed in the proposed DRI are reasonably anticipated to have an opportunity to reside within the DRI; or

- is located in an Area of Influence where the proposed DRI is reasonably anticipated to contribute to a balancing of land uses within the Area of Influence such that 25 percent of the persons who are reasonably anticipated to be employed in the proposed DRI have the opportunity to live within the Area of Influence; or

- is located in an Area of Influence with employment opportunities which are such that at least 25 percent of the persons who are reasonably anticipated to live in the proposed DRI and are reasonably expected to be employed have an opportunity to find employment appropriate to the persons' qualifications and experience within the Area of Influence (Rule Subsections 3-103.A.7.a–c).

Classifications of Large-Scale Development

During GTRA's review process, an analyst classifies the proposed DRI as one of the following four types of large-scale development:

1. Predominantly employment

2. Predominantly residential

3. Exclusively employment

4. Exclusively residential

"Exclusive" means that the entire DRI will be composed of a single-function land use (e.g., a single-family subdivision or a light industrial development). "Predominant" refers to DRIs containing more than one use but where one land use (residence or employment) dominates the land-use mix. In cases where the proposed DRI contains a mix of employment and residences, the DRI analyst will determine whether the DRI is "predominantly employment" or "predominantly residential." The analyst follows these steps when classifying DRIs:

Step 1. Estimate the labor force residing in the DRI. Determine the number of housing units to be constructed in the proposed DRI. Assume 100 percent occupancy of housing units. Multiply the number of housing units (households) by 1.5 workers per household—generally representative of national, state, and metropolitan trends in the number of workers per household—to determine the total number of residents of the proposed DRI who are in the labor force.

Step 2. Estimate employment in the DRI. Determine the number of jobs projected to be in the DRI. Calculate the amount of nonresidential building space (gross square feet), then divide that number by an acceptable standard of square footage per worker (e.g., 300 square feet per office worker and 500 square feet per retail worker).

Step 3. Compare the estimates of labor force of the proposed DRI and the number of jobs in the DRI to determine whether it is "predominantly residential" or "predominantly employment." Compare the number of residents of the proposed DRI who work with the number of jobs (employment) in the proposed DRI. If the number of residents of the DRI who work (i.e., the proposed DRI's estimated labor force) is greater than the number of jobs in the DRI, the proposed DRI is "predominantly residential." If the number of jobs (employment) in the proposed DRI exceeds the number of residents of the DRI who work, the proposed DRI is "predominantly employment" (GRTA 2003).

Data Requirements for AOI Analyses

Collecting data for analyses of jobs-housing balancing considerations can be challenging. The three AOI standards listed in the previous subsection are displayed in Table 10 in terms of data required to conduct the required analyses.

In constructing methods for these three types of analyses, criterion (c) in Table 10 (i.e., resident workers of the DRI) was most challenging in terms of compliance due to lack of employment data for small units of analysis.

Collecting data for analyses of jobs-housing balancing considerations can be challenging.

TABLE 10
ESSENTIAL DATA REQUIREMENTS FOR
NONEXPEDITED REVIEW CRITERIA 3-103.A.7

Nonexpedited Criterion 3-103.A.7	Proposed DRI		AOI	
	Detailed Data for Employment	Detailed Data for Housing	Detailed Data for Employment	Detailed Data for Housing
Proposed DRIs That Are Predominantly Employment (a. and b. shall be applied)				
a. Mix of uses (employment and housing)	Assess characteristics of workers	Assess housing opportunities in the DRI for workers working in the DRI		
b. Employees in the DRI	Assess characteristics of workers			Data on opportunity to live in AOI
Proposed DRIs That Are Predominantly Residential (a. and c. must be applied)				
a. Mix of uses (employment and housing)	Assess characteristics of workers	Assess housing opportunities in the DRI for workers working in the DRI		
c. Resident workers (employees who are residents) of the DRI	Assess characteristics of workers		Detailed data for employment	
Proposed DRIs That Are Exclusively Employment (b. must be applied)				
b. Employees in the DRI	Assess characteristics of workers			Data on opportunity to live in AOI
Proposed DRIs That Are Exclusively Residential (c. shall be applied)				
c. Resident workers (employees who are residents of the DRI	Assess characteristics of workers		Detailed data for employment	

Drawing an AOI: Geographic Unit of Analysis

The census block group is an appropriate unit of geography from which to define an AOI and for which to collect data for AOI analyses. Splitting census tracts should be avoided. The U.S. Census Bureau also provides data by traffic analysis zone (TAZ), and such data are also often available from transportation modeling data sets, such as those used by metropolitan planning organizations. A TAZ is a desirable unit of geography to use in defining and collecting data for AOIs because the area within a given TAZ is small enough to provide a reasonably reliable match to the boundaries of an AOI. The TAZ unit of geography has an advantage over the census block group in that public agencies tend to provide basic data more frequently (i.e., during intermediate years between censuses). Furthermore, TAZ data may be the only source of employment data reasonably available at the desired unit of geography.

Method of Analysis for "Predominantly Employment" or "Predominantly Residential" DRIs

As stated above, the first of GRTA's three AOI standards specifies that "the DRI contain a mix of uses which are reasonably anticipated to contribute to a balancing of land uses such that it would be affordable for at least 10 percent of the persons who are reasonably anticipated to be employed in the proposed DRI to have an opportunity to reside within the DRI" (GRTA 2002, Rule Subsection 3-103.A.7.a). The analysis is outlined in the following steps. Note that only the steps are provided here; tables and additional explanations are omitted.

- *Step 1.* Determine employment-generating land uses in the DRI.

- *Step 2.* Determine the number of workers in the DRI by type of land use and occupation.

- *Step 3.* Determine monthly salary levels for the jobs in the DRI by occupation, the monthly incomes of households (assuming 1.5 workers per household) in the DRI , and the maximum amount of income that should be spent on housing, which is 30 percent of each household's monthly salary.

- *Step 4.* Compile the household income data from Step 3 into household income ranges that will match monthly housing-cost data from the U.S. Census SF3.

- *Step 5.* Categorize the number of households living in the DRI by monthly dollar range of household income available for housing.

- *Step 6.* Determine the number of housing units that are projected to be available in the DRI by range of monthly cost (mortgage or rent).

- *Step 7.* Compare the number of households for each monthly dollar range in the DRI with the total number of housing units available in that dollar range in the DRI. Determine the difference and summarize the data results. A preferred format for presenting a summary analysis is shown in Table 11 on the opposite page.

- *Step 8.* Answer the question: Are at least 10 percent of the housing units to be provided in the DRI affordable to the households with one or more workers employed within the DRI?

TABLE 11. SUMMARY ANALYSIS OF CRITERION 3–103.A.7.A RECOMMENDED FORMAT

Monthly Dollar Range	Number of Households in the DRI That Can Afford Housing in the DRI	Number of Housing Units in the DRI	Numerical Difference of Housing Units in the DRI and the Number of Households That Can Afford Housing in the DRI	Percentage of Total Households in the DRI That Can Afford Housing in the Proposed DRI
$499 or less				
$500 to $599				
$600 to $699				
$700 to $799				
$800 to $899				
$900 to $999				
$1,000 to $1,249				
$1,250 to $1,499				
$1,500 to $1,999				
$2,000 or more				
Total				

Method of Analysis for "Predominantly Employment" or "Exclusively Employment" DRIs

The central task of this type of analysis is to compare the characteristics of workers in the DRI with housing opportunities in the AOI so as to determine whether "the DRI is located in an Area of Influence where the proposed DRI is reasonably anticipated to contribute to a balancing of land uses within the Area of Influence such that 25 percent of the persons who are reasonably anticipated to be employed in the proposed DRI have the opportunity to live within the Area of Influence" (GTRA 2002, Rule Subsection 3-103.A.7.b). The analysis outlined in the following steps should be used to verify whether a DRI meets this requirement. [Note: Steps 1–5 are the same as for the standard in the above subsection.]

- *Step 1.* Determine employment-generating land uses in the DRI.

- *Step 2.* Determine the number of workers in the DRI by type of land use and occupation.

- *Step 3.* Determine monthly salary levels for the jobs in the DRI by occupation, the monthly incomes of households (assuming 1.5 workers per household) in the DRI, and the maximum amount of income that should be spent on housing, which is 30 percent of each household's monthly salary.

- *Step 4.* Compile the household income data from Step 3 into household income ranges that will match monthly housing-cost data from the U.S. Census SF3.

- *Step 5.* Categorize the number of households living in the DRI by monthly dollar range of household income available for housing.

- *Step 6.* Determine the number of owner-occupied housing units in the AOI by selected monthly costs.

- *Step 7.* Determine the number of renter-occupied housing units in the AOI by selected monthly costs.

The central task of this type of analysis is to compare the characteristics of workers in the DRI with housing opportunities in the AOI.

- *Step 8.* Add the owner-occupied housing units and renter-occupied housing units to show the total occupied housing units in the AOI by selected monthly costs.

- *Step 9.* Compare the number of total occupied housing units by monthly costs in the AOI with the number of households that have one or more workers who work in the DRI. Determine the differences and summarize the results in a table such as Table 12.

TABLE 12. COMPARISON OF MONTHLY HOUSEHOLD INCOMES OF HOUSEHOLDS WITH ONE OR MORE WORKERS IN THE AOI WITH MONTHLY COSTS OF HOUSING UNITS IN THE AOI: RECOMMENDED FORMAT			Difference Between the Number of Occupied Housing Units in the AOI and the Number of Households With One or More Workers Working in the DRI
Monthly Dollar Range	Total Occupied Housing Units in AOI	Number of Housholds With One or More Workers Working in the DRI	
$499 or less			
$500 to $599			
$600 to $699			
$700 to $799			
$800 to $899			
$900 to $999			
$1,000 to $1,249			
$1,250 to $1,499			
$1,500 to $1,999			
$2,000 or more			
Total			

- *Step 10.* Answer the question: Do 25 percent of the persons (households) employed in the proposed DRI have the opportunity to live within the AOI?

Method of Analysis for "Predominantly Residential" or "Exclusively Residential" DRIs

The central task of this type of analysis is to compare the characteristics of residents of the DRI who work (i.e., the labor force residing in the DRI) with employment opportunities in the AOI so as to determine whether "the DRI is located in an Area of Influence with employment opportunities which are such that at least 25 percent of the persons who are reasonably anticipated to live in the proposed DRI and are reasonably expected to be employed have an opportunity to find employment appropriate to the persons' qualifications and experience within the Area of Influence" (GTRA 2002, Rule Subsection 3-103.A.7.c). The analysis outlined in the following steps should be used to verify whether a DRI meets this requirement.

- *Step 1.* Determine the total number of housing units to be provided in the DRI. This will yield a number of households.

- *Step 2.* Estimate the number of residents of the DRI who work (i.e., civilian labor force participation).

- *Step 3.* Determine the probable occupations (or qualifications and experience) of residents of the proposed DRI who work.

- *Step 4.* Estimate the number of jobs in the AOI and determine employment by occupation (or qualifications and experience) in the AOI.

- *Step 5.* Compare the occupations (or qualifications and experience) of residents of the proposed DRI who work, by occupation, with the number of jobs in the AOI, by occupation.

- *Step 6.* Answer the question: Do 25 percent or more of the residents of the DRI who are in the labor force have the opportunity to work within the AOI?

PRACTICAL CONSIDERATIONS

Balancing jobs and housing is a deceptively simple concept (Bookout 1990). Because jobs-housing balance implies that placing workers and housing closer together will reduce commuting and traffic congestion, it appears to be a simple and obvious policy to pursue (Giuliano 1991). The relationships between these variables, however, can be quite complex (Hamilton et al. 1991), as the GRTA's rules in the prior section show. And these relationships become more complex when a community tries to balance jobs and housing in practice (Clarke 1991). This section of the report addresses practical considerations such as policy formulation, legal issues, local political acceptance, and administrative and enforcement issues, as they relate to planning for and regulating jobs-housing balance.

Achieving Qualitative As Well As Quantitative Balances

A community might have an equal number of jobs and housing units but may still exhibit a mismatch between the quality of the jobs and housing units. A suburban neighborhood, for example, may have equal numbers of jobs and housing, but if the jobs are hourly service-sector positions and the housing is high-end single-family homes on large lots, the neighborhood will suffer from a qualitative jobs-housing imbalance. The type, condition, affordability, and characteristics of housing in a community, in other words, may not suit the local labor force, even if there are housing units available to labor force participants who work in that given community.

There are places where desirable jobs-housing ratios exist, but qualitative jobs-housing balances do not. Cervero (1989; 1991) found that two San Francisco Bay area communities had balanced ratios (1.3 : 1 to 1.5 : 1), but less than one-quarter of either community's residents worked within the community. Cervero (1996) also found that, despite a jobs-to-employed-residents ratio between 0.96 : 1 and 1.05 : 1, three cities in the Bay Area had fewer than 30 percent of workers residing locally and fewer than 30 percent of employed residents working locally. As another example, the San Fernando Valley was found to be balanced with respect to jobs and housing, yet in 1988, 60 percent of the traffic on local freeways started and ended someplace outside the valley (Clarke 1991).

Similarly, unbalanced jobs-housing ratios do not necessarily imply jobs-housing imbalances. The specific plan for Central City West in Los Angeles had an implicit imbalance with a 3.6 : 1 ratio. Yet suitable, close-by jobs meant that most residents were within an acceptable, lower than average, employment commute time of 15–20 minutes from their homes (Hamilton et al. 1991).

Legal Framework

As a planning tool, jobs-housing balance does not raise any significant legal issues about its applicability. Local governments are generally autho-

Balancing jobs and housing is a deceptively simple concept. . . . The relationships between these variables, however, can be quite complex.

rized to adopt comprehensive plans, and the policy content of those plans is usually left to local governments to decide, although certain state procedures and substantive requirements may apply to local comprehensive plans, as in Georgia and many other states.

Incorporating a jobs-housing policy in a comprehensive plan should be done in the context of a public process with adequate participation and debate by stakeholders about the merits of the policy. It should also identify actions needed to implement the policy. If the implementation strategy for a jobs-housing policy calls for changes to regulations in support of that policy, such regulations must be adopted under appropriate procedures that ensure due process. Any regulations must be fully justifiable with a clearly written rationale describing their public purposes. That rationale should, for example, explain how the regulation promotes the health, safety, and general welfare of the locality.

Mandatory inclusionary zoning is also generally susceptible to challenge as a regulatory taking, although some courts have upheld inclusionary zoning ordinances under regulatory takings challenges. Courts have tended to support inclusionary zoning and linkage programs only in cases where they are expressly authorized or reasonably implied by state enabling legislation (White 1992). Mandatory inclusionary housing and linkage programs might not be legally defensible in states that have no legal enabling authority.

All regulatory activities should be conducted under the guidance of the city or county attorney, as applicable.

Political Concerns and Public Acceptance

There are a number of conditions under which a jobs-housing balance can stir up public debate, if not controversy. Local elected officials are often confronted with conflicting demands from local constituents. A citizen who is opposed to change in his or her community will likely oppose any new policies, especially those that have the potential to alter something as substantial as the community's jobs-housing balance. Officials should also not assume that everyone wants to live close to his or her workplace. Individuals may not want to live and work in the same community, and consequently they may be opposed to balancing jobs and housing.

A jobs-housing balance policy, by definition, calls for an increase in housing or in employment to achieve local parity. There are numerous stakeholder groups and constituencies whose interests may be directly or indirectly affected by a jobs-housing balance policy, from restaurants that may draw more business from workers to homeowners who fear commercial development will attract crime to their neighborhood. The political environment will depend on which of the four types of jobs-housing imbalance the community is experiencing.

Type 1 imbalances. A city or county with lots of entry-level retail and service jobs but little or no low- to moderate-income housing might find it needs to correct its jobs-housing imbalance with a policy that ensures housing meets the price ranges of moderately skilled, lower-wage workers. In a wealthy bedroom community with high-amenity, suburban-style subdivisions, proposals to provide housing that introduces lower-income residents will likely face staunch opposition. Even if developers recognize that a market exists for apartments and other affordable homes in a job-rich area, their efforts to build low- to moderate-income housing can be frustrated by exclusionary zoning practices. Exclusionary zoning techniques are often adopted to block any attempt to balance existing jobs with new affordable housing units. These types of exclusionary practices often impact first-time homebuyers, younger workers, recent graduates, or senior citizens.

In a wealthy bedroom community with high-amenity, suburban-style subdivisions, proposals to provide housing that introduces lower-income residents will likely face staunch opposition.

Businesses that are experiencing labor shortages might support a jobs-housing balancing strategy designed to better satisfy the needs for housing a working population. Much of the time, members of the business community should be considered potential allies of a jobs-housing balance policy. Certain existing businesses may not support jobs recruitment, however, if the jobs sought by new businesses threaten their market shares.

Type 2 imbalances. A community might find that it needs more high-end residences to house corporate executives and similar high-income professionals. Due to the substantial market demand and the high profits developers draw from new subdivisions targeted at these professionals, however, shortages of high-end housing are rare. Exceptions typically exist in a central-city area that has not established an in-town residential market. In this case, a local government would be wise to begin by performing market research to identify the barriers to market-rate housing, such as a lack of amenities, perceived low quality of public schools, or concern about crime. Introducing upper-income housing in downtowns with a tight housing market must be done carefully with much community input, or it can have undesirable effects, such as displacing urban poor through gentrification. In general, however, local governments will find it easier to secure community approval for higher-end housing than moderate- or low-income housing.

Type 3 imbalances. If it is necessary to bring industrial, storage, trucking, and warehousing types of jobs to a community in order to eliminate a blue-collar job deficiency, such heavy commercial and light industrial uses may not be acceptable to the city or county because the locality may not have the infrastructure requirements or the vacant land to supply them. Neighborhood groups often oppose new development for these uses due to noise, odor, and other off-site impacts. But other types of new employment, such as service, retail, or professional jobs, may not fit the characteristics of the existing residents. Communities that want the additional blue-collar employment provided by companies that may have off-site impacts can mitigate those impacts with performance standards (see Schwab 1993).

Type 4 imbalances. Employers study the strength of the local labor force in terms of workers' skills and education levels and thus tend to locate where highly skilled labor exists. Economic development strategies that seek to capture employers offering jobs with high skill levels are rarely controversial, although "no growth" or "slow growth" advocates might object. Generally, it is easier for a city or county to attract nonresidential development because of the perception (or, in some cases, the reality) that nonresidential development is a net tax generator when compared with the municipal or county services it requires. For these reasons, communities with deficiencies in skilled jobs are far more likely to accept a jobs-housing balancing policy.

Administrative Complexity

As with the legal and political considerations described above, the administrative requirements needed to implement a jobs-housing balance will vary depending on the approach selected. The most difficult task about a jobs-housing balance policy is determining a standard that expresses what the community wants and then gaining consensus for adoption of that standard. As a planning tool, making the concept of jobs-housing balance operational involves several fairly complex considerations. Generally, the more sophisticated the method for determining and achieving jobs-housing balance becomes, the more complex, time consuming, and subjective it is to implement.

Determining qualitative and quantitative balances between jobs and housing often requires a more elaborate set of data than now exists for

Introducing upper-income housing in downtowns with a tight housing market must be done carefully with much community input, or it can have undesirable effects, such as displacing urban poor through gentrification.

most communities. For instance, if a local government wants to balance quantitatively the jobs and housing in a subarea of a city or county, it might find that data are not readily available and therefore must be compiled for the new unit of geography. Regional commissions typically prepare annual housing and employment estimates for census tracts. These commissions may also have small area estimates of households and employment that are prepared for regional transportation models and tabulated for traffic analysis zones (TAZs). These data sources can also be very helpful in providing documentation for a jobs-housing balance policy. For more information on the reliability and application of these subarea data sources, see the section above on applying the jobs-housing policy in large-scale development review.

Jurisdictions that want to qualitatively balance jobs and housing must do extensive research and must conduct analyses to learn which types and costs of housing units most closely match the needs and demands of area labor force participants. Finding this qualitative balance is, however, an inexact science, as much of the jobs-housing balance literature shows. On the other hand, local governments that want to know in general terms how jobs and housing compare quantitatively in their jurisdictions can study existing data on the total numbers of jobs and housing units. These general numbers can indicate at minimum whether a community needs more jobs or more housing to achieve a balance.

Cost of Implementation

The costs of adopting a jobs-housing balance policy are, simply, whatever costs are necessary to prepare, adopt, and implement the policy through administrative or regulatory means. Like all other legal, political, and administrative matters, these costs will differ depending on the intensiveness of the approach used. A comprehensive plan amendment that adopts a new jobs-housing balance policy will take staff time to prepare, and existing staff may or may not have time to devote to a careful study of the jobs-housing balance issue. Counties and cities with long-range planning staffs should be able to conduct jobs-housing balance studies without additional personnel, particularly if simpler quantitative measures are used. In cases where existing planning staff members do not have sufficient time, or a more sophisticated study is desired, additional assistance from a consultant or regional commission may be needed.

Community consensus on a jobs-housing balance policy can be an elusive goal. Achieving a job-housing balance is a mid- to long-term community goal and therefore should be considered whenever incremental changes are made in the community. If major changes in the community fabric are implied by a particular jobs-housing balance policy, local governments should expect to spend much time (and money) to explain, debate, revise, and build consent for the new policy. Local city or county planning staffs may or may not be in a position to take on these responsibilities; if not, they should consider professionally facilitated sessions, public hearings, and community workshops, all, of course, at potentially substantial costs.

There are some cost efficiencies possible if a community incorporates its study and implementation of jobs-housing balance into a more general update of its comprehensive plan. If the community knows it wants to consider or pursue a jobs-housing balance policy, collecting the necessary data at the same time as other economic development and housing data are compiled can reduce costs of data collection and analysis. Also, local governments that have access to TAZ data via a transportation modeling process can reduce costs by using housing and employment estimates from that work.

Achieving a job-housing balance is a mid- to long-term community goal and therefore should be considered whenever incremental changes are made in the community.

CONCLUDING OBSERVATIONS

- Jobs-housing techniques are best developed not in isolation, but rather as part of another study or program, such as smart growth efforts, housing task forces or reports, economic development efforts, general growth forecasting studies, or transportation plans. It is also most cost-efficient to undertake a jobs-housing analysis as a part of another study or planning effort.

- Jobs-housing balance should be considered a mid- to long-range goal that the community can achieve incrementally through various local actions over time.

- Let data availability guide your choice of methods for measuring jobs-housing balance as well as of the area you are measuring, unless you have an interest in a particular aspect of jobs-housing balance that justifies extra data-gathering effort.

- Use housing and employment data by traffic analysis zone (TAZ), if available, or census block group to calculate jobs-housing ratios in sub-areas of a jurisdiction.

- When arguing in favor of a jobs-housing balance policy, be sure to note that such a policy does not necessarily imply higher densities—that is, jobs-housing balance policies are "density neutral." Jobs-housing policies only suggest that a given geographic area ought to have both jobs and housing.

- Qualitative factors should be considered in addition to quantitative factors.

- A jobs-housing balance strategy is a primary method to support regional transportation and development goals.

REFERENCES

Altshuler, Alan A., and Jose A. Gomez-Ibanez. 1993. *Regulation for Revenue: The Political Economy of Land Use Exactions.* Washington, D.C.: Brookings Institution.

Armstrong, Michael, and Brett Sears. 2001. "The New Economy and Jobs/Housing Balance in Southern California." Southern California Association of Governments. April. Also available at http://www.scag.ca.gov/housing/jobhousing/balance.html.

Atlanta Regional Commission. 2002. *Community Choices Quality Growth Toolkit: Jobs-Housing Balance.* [Accessed October 2002]. Available at http://www.atlreg.com/qualitygrowth/planning/toolkits/jobs_housing_balance_tool.pdf.

Beauregard, Robert A. 1995. "Edge Cities: Peripheralizing the Center." *Urban Geography* 16, no. 8: 708–721.

Benfield, F. Kaid, Matthew D. Raimi, and Donald D. T. Chen. 1999. *Once There Were Greenfields: How Urban Sprawl Is Undermining America's Environment, Economy, and Social Fabric.* New York: Natural Resources Defense Council.

Binger, Gary. 2001. "Jobs/Housing Balance: Strategies for California." Southern California Real Estate Summit Brief Series. Urban Land Institute District Council, Los Angeles and Lusk Center for Real Estate, University of Southern California. September 13. Also available at http://www.usc.edu/schools/sppd/lusk/professional/summit/2001/pdf/jobshousingII.pdf.

Bookout, Lloyd W. 1990. "Jobs and Housing: The Search For Balance." *Urban Land* 49, no. 10: 5–9.

Boulder, City of, Planning and Public Works. n.d. Attachment B: Background of the Jobs/Housing Project.[Accessed August 22, 2003.] Available at http://www.ci.boulder.co.us/buildingservices/jobs_to_pop/documents/AttachmentB.pdf.

Brookings Institution Center on Urban and Metropolitan Policy. 2000. *Moving Beyond Sprawl: The Challenge for Metropolitan Atlanta*. Washington, D.C.: Brookings Institution.

California Department of Housing and Community Development. 2000. "Inter-Regional Partnership (IRP) Grants for Jobs-Housing Balance." [Accessed at http://www.hcd.ca.gov/ca/irpgjhb/]. No longer available.

Cervero, Robert. 1989. "Jobs-Housing Balancing and Regional Mobility." *Journal of the American Planning Association* 55, no. 2: 139–150.

-------. 1991. "Jobs/Housing Balance as Public Policy." *Urban Land* 50, no. 10: 10–14.

-------. 1996. "Jobs-Housing Balance Revisited: Trends and Impacts in the San Francisco Bay Area." *Journal of the American Planning Association* 62, no. 4: 492–511.

Choo, Sangho, Patricia L. Mokhtarian, and Ilan Salomon. 2001. "Impacts of Telecommuting on Vehicle-Miles Traveled: A Nationwide Time Series Analysis." Consultant Report P600-01-020, California Energy Commission. December. Also available at http://www.energy.ca.gov/reports/2002-01-30_600-01-20.PDF.

Clarke, Paul. 1991. "Developments: Balancing Jobs and Housing in the San Fernando Valley." *Urban Land* 50, no. 2: 26.

DeChiara, Joseph, Julius Panero, and Martin Zelnick. 1995. *Time-Saver Standards for Housing and Residential Development*. 2nd ed. New York: McGraw-Hill.

Downs, Anthony. 1992. *Stuck in Traffic: Coping With Peak Hour Traffic Congestion*. Washington, D.C., and Cambridge, Mass.: Brookings Institution and the Lincoln Institute of Land Policy.

Economic Development Council of Seattle and King County. 2003. "Are We Growing Smart? No." [Accessed August 22, 2003.] Available at http://www.edc-sea.org/about/smartgrowth/#bal.

Ewing, Reid. 1996. *Best Development Practices: Doing the Right Thing and Making Money at the Same Time*. Chicago: Planners Press.

Frank, Lawrence, and Gary Pivo. 1994. *Relationships Between Land Use and Travel Behavior in the Puget Sound Region*. Seattle: Washington State Transportation Center.

Garreau, Joel. 1991. *Edge City: Life on the New Frontier*. New York: Doubleday.

Georgia Department of Community Affairs. 2003. "Rules of Georgia Department of Community Affairs, Chapter 110-12-1 Minimum Standards and Procedures for Local Planning. Effective January 1, 2004." Also available at http://www.dca.state.ga.us/planning/OCP_Rules/RevMinimumStandards120402.pdf.

Georgia Regional Transportation Authority. 2002. Procedures and Principles for GRTA Development of Regional Impact Review. Adopted January 14. Also available at http://www.grta.org/dri/PDF_files/DRI_Procedures_Principles_FINAL_112901.pdf.

Giuliano, Genevieve. 1991. "Is Jobs-Housing Balance a Transportation Issue?" *Transportation Research Record,* no. 1305: 305–12.

Hamilton, Edward K., Francine F. Rabinovitz, John H. Alschuler, Jr., and Paul J. Silvern. 1991. "Applying the Jobs/Housing Balance Concept." *Urban Land* 50, no. 10: 15–18.

Lane Council of Governments. 2000. "Examining the Public Sector Role in the Regional Distribution of Jobs and Housing." Region 2050. September 6. Also available at http://www.region2050.org/pdf/meetings/jobshous2.pdf.

LeGates, Richard T. 2001. "Housing Incentives to Promote Inter-regional Jobs/Housing Balance." [Accessed August 22, 2003.] Available at http://www.abag.ca.gov/planning/interregional/pdf/housing_incentives.pdf.

Levine, Jonathan. 1998. "Rethinking Accessibility and Jobs-Housing Balance." *Journal of the American Planning Association* 64, no. 2: 133–49.

Meck, Stuart, Rebecca Retzlaff, and James Schwab. 2003. *Regional Approaches to Affordable Housing*. Planning Advisory Service Report No. 513/514. Chicago: American Planning Association.

Metro. 1994a. "Concepts for Growth: Report to Council." Portland, Ore.

-------. 1994b. *Recommended Alternative Decision Kit*. Portland, Ore.: Metro.

Moore, Terry, and Paul Thorsnes. 1994. *The Transportation/Land Use Connection*. Planning

Advisory Service Report No. 448/449. Chicago: American Planning Association.

Nationwide Personal Transportation Survey. 2000. "U.S. Personal Travel per Household, Driver, and Mode, 1969, 1977, 1983, 1990, and 1995." [Accessed August 21, 2003]. Available at http://ceq.eh.doe.gov/nepa/reports/statistics/tab10x4.html.

Nowlan, David M., and Greg Stewart. 1991. "Downtown Population Growth and Commuting Trips: Recent Experience in Toronto." *Journal of the American Planning Association* 57, no. 2: 165–182.

Porter, Douglas R. 1997. *Managing Growth in America's Communities.* Washington, D.C.: Island Press.

Schwab, Jim. 1993. *Industrial Performance Standards for a New Century.* Planning Advisory Service Report No. 444. Chicago: American Planning Association.

Siebert, Trent. 2003. "Cities Seek to Keep Workers Near Home: Regional Planners Target 'Jobs/Housing Balance.'" *Denver Post,* January 13, 1A.

Sierra Business Council. 1999. "Assembly Select Committee on Jobs-Housing Balance Moves Ahead." [Accessed August 22, 2003.] Available at http://www.sbcouncil.org/news/winter 99/iii.htm#2.

Stover, Vergil G., and Frank J. Koepke. 1988. *Transportation and Land Development.* Englewood Cliffs, N.J.: Prentice-Hall for Institute of Transportation Engineers.

Texas Transportation Institute. 2001. "Appendix B: Methodology for 2002 Annual Report." In 2002 Urban Mobility Study. Also available at http://mobility.tamu.edu/ums/study/methods/entire_methodology.pdf.

Urban Land Institute. 1999. *Smart Growth: Myth and Fact.* Washington, D.C.: Urban Land Institute.

Washington Research Council. 2000. "Living On the Teeter-Totter: The Balance Between Jobs & Housing in King County." Special Report, Washington Research Council. December 29. Also available at http://www.researchcouncil.org/Reports/2000/JobsHousing1/KingCoJobsHousingBal.pdf.

Weitz, Jerry. 2003. "Whither the Planned Unit Development?" *Practicing Planner* 1, no. 1.

-------. 1999. *Sprawl Busting: State Programs to Guide Growth.* Chicago: Planners Press.

Weitz, Jerry, and Tim Schindler. 1997. "Are Oregon's Communities Balanced? A Test of the Jobs-Housing Balance Policy and the Impact of Balance on Mean Commute Times." Unpublished manuscript. Department of Urban Studies and Planning, Portland State University.

Weitz, Jerry, and Leora Susan Waldner. 2002. *Smart Growth Audits.* Planning Advisory Service Report No. 512. Chicago: American Planning Association.

White, S. Mark. 1992. *Affordable Housing: Proactive and Reactive Strategies.* Planning Advisory Service Report No. 441. Chicago: American Planning Association.

Wunder, Charles. 2000. *Regulating Home-Based Businesses in the Twenty-First Century.* Planning Advisory Service Report No. 499. Chicago: American Planning Association.

464. Planners' Salaries and Employment Trends. Marya Morris. July 1996. 25pp.

465. Adequate Public Facilities Ordinances and Transportation Management. S. Mark White. August 1996. 80pp.

466. Planning for Hillside Development. Robert B. Olshansky. November 1996. 50pp.

467. A Planners Guide to Sustainable Development. Kevin J. Krizek and Joe Power. December 1996. 66pp.

468. Creating Transit-Supportive Land-Use Regulations. Marya Morris, ed. December 1996. 76pp.

469. Gambling, Economic Development, and Historic Preservation. Christopher Chadbourne, Philip Walker, and Mark Wolfe. March 1997. 56pp.

470/471. Habitat Protection Planning: Where the Wild Things Are. Christopher J. Duerksen, Donald L. Elliott, N. Thompson Hobbs, Erin Johnson, and James R. Miller. May 1997. 82pp.

472. Converting Storefronts to Housing: An Illustrated Guide. July 1997. 88pp.

473. Subdivision Design in Flood Hazard Areas. Marya Morris. September 1997. 62pp.

474/475. Online Resources for Planners. Sanjay Jeer. November 1997. 126pp.

476. Nonpoint Source Pollution: A Handbook for Local Governments. Sanjay Jeer, Megan Lewis, Stuart Meck, Jon Witten, and Michelle Zimet. December 1997. 127pp.

477. Transportation Demand Management. Erik Ferguson. March 1998. 68pp.

478. Manufactured Housing: Regulation, Design Innovations, and Development Options. Welford Sanders. July 1998. 120pp.

479. The Principles of Smart Development. September 1998. 113pp.

480/481. Modernizing State Planning Statutes: The Growing Smart^SM Working Papers. Volume 2. September 1998. 269pp.

482. Planning and Zoning for Concentrated Animal Feeding Operations. Jim Schwab. December 1998. 44pp.

483/484. Planning for Post-Disaster Recovery and Reconstruction. Jim Schwab, et al. December 1998. 346pp.

485. Traffic Sheds, Rural Highway Capacity, and Growth Management. Lane Kendig with Stephen Tocknell. March 1999. 24pp.

486. Youth Participation in Community Planning. Ramona Mullahey, Yve Susskind, and Barry Checkoway. June 1999. 70pp.

489/490. Aesthetics, Community Character, and the Law. Christopher J. Duerksen and R. Matthew Goebel. December 1999. 154pp.

493. Transportation Impact Fees and Excise Taxes: A Survey of 16 Jurisdictions. Connie Cooper. July 2000. 62pp.

494. Incentive Zoning: Meeting Urban Design and Affordable Housing Objectives. Marya Morris. September 2000. 64pp.

495/496. Everything You Always Wanted To Know About Regulating Sex Businesses. Eric Damian Kelly and Connie Cooper. December 2000. 168pp.

497/498. Parks, Recreation, and Open Spaces: An Agenda for the 21st Century. Alexander Garvin. December 2000. 72pp.

499. Regulating Home-Based Businesses in the Twenty-First Century. Charles Wunder. December 2000. 37pp.

500/501. Lights, Camera, Community Video. Cabot Orton, Keith Spiegel, and Eddie Gale. April 2001. 76pp.

502. Parks and Economic Development. John L. Crompton. November 2001. 74pp.

503/504. Saving Face: How Corporate Franchise Design Can Respect Community Identity (revised edition). Ronald Lee Fleming. February 2002. 118pp.

505. Telecom Hotels: A Planners Guide. Jennifer Evans-Crowley. March 2002. 31pp.

506/507. Old Cities/Green Cities: Communities Transform Unmanaged Land. J. Blaine Bonham, Jr., Gerri Spilka, and Darl Rastorfer. March 2002. 123pp.

508. Performance Guarantees for Government Permit Granting Authorities. Wayne Feiden and Raymond Burby. July 2002. 80pp.

509. Street Vending: A Survey of Ideas and Lessons for Planners. Jennifer Ball. August 2002. 44pp.

510/511. Parking Standards. Edited by Michael Davidson and Fay Dolnick. November 2002. 181pp.

512. Smart Growth Audits. Jerry Weitz and Leora Susan Waldner. November 2002. 56pp.

513/514. Regional Approaches to Affordable Housing. Stuart Meck, Rebecca Retzlaff, and James Schwab. February 2003. 271pp.

515. Planning for Street Connectivity: Getting from Here to There. Susan Hardy, Robert G. Paterson, and Kent Butler. May 2003. 95pp.

516. Jobs-Housing Balance. Jerry Weitz. November 2003. 41pp.